How to Make Notes and Write

# HOW TO MAKE NOTES AND WRITE

Formerly A Short Handbook for Writing Essays in the Humanities and Social Sciences

Dan Allosso and S. F. Allosso

Bemidji, Minnesota

How to Make Notes and Write by Dan Allosso is licensed under a Creative Commons Attribution-NonCommercial-ShareAlike 4.0 International License, except where otherwise noted.

# CONTENTS

Introduction                                              1

I.   **Main Body**
1.   Inspiration, Interest, Anxiety                       5
2.   Writing is Thinking                                 14
3.   Working with Ideas                                  23
4.   Highlighting and Taking Notes                       33
5.   Making Source Notes                                 44
6.   Discovering Topics and Connections                  58
7.   Organizing Output                                   69
8.   Coherent Paragraphs                                 81
9.   Effective Sentences                                 95
10.  Appropriate Words                                  107
11.  Revising                                           116

Revision Checklist                                      127
Exercises                                               129

# INTRODUCTION

Why should you read a book about Note-making and Writing? Why this book?

Hi! I'm Dan Allosso. I'm a History professor, so it would be accurate to say that I make notes and write for a living. It's my second career (my first was in technology), so it would also be fair to say it's an avocation as well as a vocation. Something I do because I really love it; not just to pay the bills.

If you are a student, I hope you're studying something that truly excites you and makes you happy at the same time it does some good in the world. If you're older, I hope you're pursuing something that interests you, whether for work or as a "hobby". There's a long tradition of people who did their music or art or writing in their spare time while holding down a "day job". In either case, the techniques you'll learn in this book will help you make the most of your efforts. And even if you're not (yet) on a path where you're following your own interests and are only looking for tips on how to get more from your work on school assignments, you've come to the right place. You might even find, once making notes and writing your thoughts becomes much easier and more effective, that it's something you'll return to just for the fun of it!

This book began its life as "A Short Handbook for Writing Essays in the Humanities", written by my father, Dr. S. F. Allosso, a literature teacher at the University of California. It was designed to be a brief and practical tool to help his students read literature and write an essay. When he retired and I became a teacher, I picked it up and added some ideas and examples from History. Again, the idea was to help students who arrived in my classes with a wide variety of practice writing.

Over the last few years, one of the topics I've been interested in, outside of work, has been something called "personal knowledge management". This is a set of techniques that has some people so excited they've begun calling it by the acronym PKM. Often, a lot of this excitement comes from the technologies people have developed to make note-taking more automated and efficient. As a former techie, I'm not immune to geeking out over a great new app. You'll read about several in this book, that I use daily and also introduce to my students. The point of these tools, I want to point out, is not themselves and their capabilities, but the work they help us do.

The excitement over PKM has spilled over into blogs, YouTube channels, online courses, and books. Like other productivity hacks of the past (*The One Minute Manager*, *Getting Things Done*, etc.), techniques such as "Linking Your Thinking", "Writing Smart Notes", or "Building a Second Brain" contain a lot of useful ideas and have sometimes launched careers for their authors. These brand-name systems promise to pull together all the information you're pursuing, organize it, and connect it to your life in ways that will make you more effective as a student or professional.

This is an admirable goal. I've read all these books and watched these videos with interest. I've found a lot of good material in them that has helped me improve my workflow as I'm reading, listening to podcasts, watching videos, attending meetings and conferences, and writing about what I've learned. I suspect, however, that not everyone is as excited about the details of PKM as I have been. Many people want to invest their time actually learning new things rather than trying new apps. Many students want to get better at remembering and understanding the things they've learned — and yes, writing papers about them. If you're one of these people, this book is for you.

First, we'll cover techniques (and a few tools) you can use to turn what you're reading, watching, and hearing into useable information. This process has as much to do with taking ownership of ideas as it does with apps. Second, we'll look at how you can organize and link ideas to make them useful to you and direct them at new questions. Third, and maybe most important, we'll focus on how you get that information back *out of* your notes and into a form you can use to share your ideas with others.

# 1

# INSPIRATION, INTEREST, ANXIETY

### Inspiration and Interest (A new project! YES!)

Although probably no one is immune from anxiety, many creative people feel excitement and anticipation at the thought of a new project. We find inspiration and a rush of energy as we begin a big writing project. There's a saying, though, that you make your own luck. This book will show you several practical ways of improving your odds of being inspired when you're beginning to write.

We've all heard stories of bestselling authors and brilliant academics who outproduced their rivals in books and articles. What you might not know is that several of these overachievers held themselves to a strict rule of never doing any writing that they were not feeling excited about. How could this be? Here are a couple of examples.

Dr. Niklas Luhmann was one of the foremost European sociologists of the twentieth century and the author of about sixty books and 500 journal articles. Despite being one of the most prolific authors in his field, Luhmann famously once said he never forced himself to do anything he didn't like. Similarly, bestselling author Nassim Nicholas Taleb claims that he only writes when he wants, about topics that interest him. If he's bored with a topic, Taleb says, then his reader will most likely be bored with it too. Taleb believes he's doing both himself and his reader a favor, not forcing himself to slog through material he isn't excited writing. In general, I agree, but I have a couple of thoughts about this.

While the type of advice that says things like "follow your bliss" or "do what you love and the money will follow" is inspirational and has important elements of truth in it about both motivation and ultimate happiness with your life, often you have to do things because you have to do them. We're not always in control of our environments to the extent where we can say, "yeah, I'm not feeling it today so I don't think I'll do this assignment." This is especially true for students.

Taleb is independently wealthy. He apparently made a lot of money in the market betting against the "suckers" who didn't see one of the last market bubbles, in the way he describes in his books on "black swans" and "antifragility". While this success validates his thesis and lends additional credibility to his arguments, it also makes him fundamentally different from those of us who still work for a living or study to gain a degree so we can begin working for a living. Taleb writes to please himself, because he has already paid his bills. This allows him to project an attitude that has become a bit of a trademark for him.

Luhmann, similarly, was already over-achieving when he said he didn't force himself to write when he wasn't feeling it. He was a tenured professor at a prestigious European university with a ridiculous publishing record. If we were already producing at a very high level and doing way more than what was asked of us, then we would be freer to set the terms of our work. But it may be worth asking, which is the chicken and which the egg?

In the United States, Luhmann is best known for a note-taking method he developed called *Zettelkasten*, which you'll read more about very shortly. Although many of the techniques he used date back centuries, Luhmann put them together into a system that worked very well for him and allowed him to accumulate over ninety thousand cross-referenced notes during the course of his career. He did so much work, reading and taking notes on subjects that interested him, that topics for articles and monographs just seemed to jump out of his note boxes. The actual writing, he claimed, was the easy part.

Unlike Taleb or Luhmann, today's students are typically confronted with a new set of information each semester, often from different fields of study. It's no surprise, really, that they may not feel as motivated as people who have had the time and freedom to choose their topics. It doesn't take a lot of will power to work on something you like, or even love. Is there a way we can take advantage of some of that energy, and make it easier on ourselves by following our interests?

Often, in the humanities and social sciences, there is a set of information with which we're supposed to be engaging. But there are usually a number of ways we can do this; a number of paths through the maze of textbooks, sources, and lectures. It's very unlikely, if you pick up your classmate's copy of the textbook you're both reading, that all your highlights and notes will be identical. The things that interested you will probably be even more diverse if the class is reading a novel! Similarly, if I'm lecturing on the first World War, I'll probably want you to remember that it was fought from 1914 to 1919. But there are nearly an infinite number of ways to understand and talk about WWI. Some historians have looked at the ways the war changed culture and helped produce a "modern crisis", while others have studied the battles. Still others have focused on political, environmental, or social histories of the war years, or the experiences of different groups of people such as women, minorities, or subjects of colonial powers. So there's a lot of wiggle room even within an assigned topic. If you can latch onto an aspect or element of the assigned material that interests you, you'll nearly always be able to find something relevant to say in a class discussion, on an exam, or in an essay that will satisfy your instructor.

And frequently, the topic will actually be up to you. In many classes, students are given a chance to choose a topic for a term paper, within a range of possibilities. This is a huge opportunity to follow your interests and research something that you feel curious or passionate about. Teachers prefer to read exam essays and term papers about topics that interested the writer. As Taleb observed, if you're bored with it and just going through the motions, it will show.

Finally, returning to the example of Luhmann, it helps a lot to be over-prepared. It is much easier to write when you don't have to "brainstorm" to come up with a topic. There may be some subjects where it really makes sense to memorize facts from flash-cards; but probably not as many as we think. The reason so many writers take inspiration from the German sociologist is that he was never at a loss for things to write about. His box of notes was full of information and the connections he made while reading and researching, which were captured in those notes, actually *showed him what he had found interesting* as he was reading. According to his own statements and reports of people who observed his work, Luhmann had enough notes in his box that he was able to work on a number of projects simultaneously and jump from one to another as the spirit moved him. This technique also allowed him to discover connections between different research topics or themes of his studies, which led to insights that people who were not so well-prepared wouldn't have been able to discover. So that's our aim here: to create a system for ourselves that will make it easier for us to understand what we're reading and hearing in our studies. That will make the course content more memorable, better connected, and easier to use. And also more fun.

### Anxiety (A new project? No!)

Not everyone feels a rush of energy with each new project. And even those who do, don't always. Anxiety can be the writer's first obstacle, and this feeling is not necessarily restricted to brand new writers! We sometimes wonder, "what can I write about this topic that hasn't already been written by someone else, and probably much better than I'll be able to do it?" The fear of a blank screen (it used to be a pristine, white page of paper in a notebook or blank new sheet inserted into a typewriter) has haunted experienced writers as well as first-timers. But this anxiety, sometimes called writer's block, is not insurmountable, for brand new writers or for old veterans.

Writer's block is most often a reaction to not being entirely prepared. It's not the same as fatigue, although exhaustion is sometimes mistaken for writer's block at the end of a semester when a big research paper is due. One way to break through the anxiety is to begin writing! As you can see, the author of this handbook is already on the way to overcoming any fears he may have had, getting started on this chapter, simply by writing a couple of pages. Often, we know more about a topic than we realize, and we discover that by writing. However, good authors are usually still a bit anxious about doing a good job and making their work something useful or enjoyable, that you'll benefit from reading.

As the example of discovering what we know by writing illustrates, writing is thinking. Many people seem to believe that in order for it to count, you have to do your thinking *in your head* and only write down your thoughts once they are fully formulated and ready to be read by others. This may be the case for some writers, but none I've ever met! The two authors who have contributed to this text have over a century of writing experience between us. For us and for most of the other writers we know, the best way to discover and refine what we think is to write about it. Some of what we write may only be meaningful to ourselves. But even these private notes and lists and questions are a vital part of the process. We'll return to explore this in more detail, soon.

Writing about anything – a novel, a historical primary source, an exam question – is at least a three-way dialogue. In the case of this handbook the conversation is between me, the writer; you, the reader; and the material. Similarly, writing about something you have read or researched should serve at least three purposes: to explore the material; to describe your reactions to it; and to communicate with *your* reader.

Waiting to begin reading, researching, making notes, and writing until you know exactly what and how you want to write is unproductive. You learn by writing. The way you begin writing notes, observations, and ideas may not resemble the final form of the output you want to create. And the ideas, interpretations, and themes on which you end up concentrating may also not be what you had originally anticipated. Don't worry about that. Stay open to discovery.

Writing is a craft for most of us, not an art. This is not only an appropriate level of modesty for those of us who are more interested in communicating effectively than winning the Nobel Prize for literature; it is also very liberating. It means we are not seeking perfection and we don't have to wait until everything is flawless before we let anyone see our work. It also means that like any other skill in the world, we learn by practicing.

Sounds simple enough, doesn't it? Then why bother to state the obvious? Because new (and even some old) writers have often absorbed myths about writing that get in their way. And because some writing manuals assume new writers know things that they don't, because their authors have known those things for so long. It can be very difficult, when you've been doing something daily for decades, to remember what it was like to learn the basics for the first time. One way to be reminded of this, though, is to work with students while they are learning these basics. One of this handbook's contributors taught high school English and then University Literature classes for about forty years. The current author (his son), has been teaching undergraduate History for about ten years. This handbook will take you step-by-step through the process of making effective notes on readings and research, organizing those notes into ideas and interpretations of your own, and writing an essay for a college course or an article for general readers. The handbook will use examples from literature and history, because one of us is a History professor and the other was a master teacher of Literature.

The advice you'll find here will be relatively basic and direct, because most college essays or writing for general readers should be basic and direct. Remember, this is utilitarian writing, not poetry or the great American novel. You're probably reading this handbook either because it has been assigned or because you've realized you need some help developing these skills (good for you!). Even so, to hold your interest, this book needs to get to the point. Nothing turns away readers as quickly as feeling that their time is being wasted. Therefore, just like you, I need to decide how best to use the time and space I've been given for this task. What words to use? What tone to set? How to organize the writing so that it makes sense and gets the job done; and so the reader feels the least possible amount of pain – or maybe even has some fun? These are all questions I'm asking myself as I outline, draft, and revise this handbook. These are the questions the handbook will help you ask and answer about your own writing.

# 2

# WRITING IS THINKING

> *He who understands also loves, notices, sees...the more knowledge is inherent in a thing, the greater the love.* Paracelsus (1493-1541)

> *Now, a few words on looking for things. When you go looking for something specific, your chances of finding it are very bad, because of all the things in the world, you're only looking for one of them. When you go looking for anything at all, your chances of finding it are very good, because of all the things in the world, you're sure to find some of them.* (*The Zero Effect*, 1998)

I've already said this, but it is a key point so I'll repeat it here. In a very real way, writing is thinking. Neuroscientists believe we can only keep about seven thoughts in our attention or short term memory. Worse, they also say the "window of consciousness" during which we can focus on a particular thought is only about seven seconds. The exception to this limit, historically, has been when we are talking to someone else. In prehistory, before writing, talking was thinking. Today, writing has taken the place of talking. Some people see this as a loss, but it may be a bit safer. While it may be possible to talk without thinking, it is probably more difficult to write without thinking.

Writing an idea down in a way that makes sense is how we determine that we have really understood a topic or a point. It is also the first step in making that idea our own. Although we will continue to give the originators of ideas credit with appropriate citation (just as *they* did, before us, with their source), when we can express an idea in our own words, it's on the way to becoming ours.

You've probably often heard that the way to test your knowledge of something is to teach it to someone else. This is the same concept, but earlier in the process. There are several stages of this process and as you move through them the ideas will become progressively more your own, because you'll be progressing from recording data to interpreting that information and making it relevant to your own interests or project.

Generally, the steps in the process of making information into knowledge are:

1. Highlight a text, take notes on a lecture, video, or other source, or record ideas as they come to you;
2. Summarize and paraphrase (and only rarely quote) this information into a Source Note;

3. Engage with the idea and comment or elaborate on it in a Point Note.

I've capitalized the names of these notes because there is a lot of energy devoted to naming the different types of notes and the workflows they represent. As I mentioned, the sociologist Niklas Luhmann (1927-1998) developed a technique called *Zettelkasten*, which is a German word meaning "box of notes". He wrote a couple of articles about his process, and said in one of them, "It is impossible to think without writing." He seemed to realize this was a reach, so he immediately qualified the statement and continued, "at least, it is impossible in any sophisticated or *anschlußfähig* fashion." The German word can be translated as "connectable", but many readers today say "networked".

Several other scholars have written more about it since his death. One of these, an educational researcher named Sönke Ahrens, wrote a bestseller in 2017 that was titled *How to Take Smart Notes* in English but *Das Zettelkasten-Prinzip* in German. As you would expect from that title, the book is Ahrens' attempt to translate Luhmann's technique into non-academic English, and also to make it compatible with a range of new digital applications. An entire genre of personal knowledge management has blossomed on YouTube, reddit, in blogs, and even in online courses, known by its fans as PKM. In addition to *zettel*, some of the other names used for various types of notes are, Fleeting Note, Literature Note, Reading Note, Permanent Note, Evergreen Note, Main Note, and Atomic Note.

A lot has been written about how each of these notes should be structured; most of which I *did not* find particularly helpful in helping me get to output. What *has helped* me get to output is being able to find the ideas I'm looking for and see how I have connected them to other ideas over time. Different types of output call for different combinations of evidence, argument, and narrative. I don't think it is particularly important to know what type of note we are writing at any given time. We're in a process of gradually turning ideas we discover in sources into our own thoughts. Some of the notes I write are more about the sources. I call those Source Notes. Some are a bit more about the train of thought I'm developing. I call those Point Notes. They live side by side in the same file drawers, and I use them in output when they're appropriate.

Apps such as Zotero, Roam Research, Notion, Evernote, Obsidian, The Brain, mymind, OneNote, SimpleNote, Bear, Notability, MarginNote, and many others have jumped onto that "networked" statement Luhmann made and claim to be the best way to make and organize notes. Many of them are useful for particular tasks. None of them I have tried so far does *everything* I want to do. Sometimes excitement over the "shininess" of a new app has caused me to try to use it for things it really isn't suited for or to try to change my workflow to fit the tool. This has always turned out to be a mistake. Finally, some critics of excessive automation argue that too much technology may actually get in the way of understanding and insight. I suspect the best toolset varies based on the specific job you are trying to do and your own preferences and tech skills. I'll focus on demonstrating the workflow in the old-fashioned, paper-and-pen format and try to avoid taking sides. I still use several apps, but I try to use them only where they improve the quality of my output or my ease in creating output.

Over time I think we will all find a combination of tools and develop a hybrid system that works best for our purposes.

Far more important than what these notes are called is *what they do* in helping you make the transition from acquiring information from others to making it your own. The most basic of these techniques is a simple highlight of what jumped out at you from a text. This is the first stage of filtering. Maybe the "To Be or Not to Be" speech in *Hamlet* didn't really spark your interest that much, but the prince's treatment of Rosencrantz and Guildenstern left you with thoughts and questions. In the second stage, which I call a Source Note, you'll summarize and paraphrase the passage that grabbed your attention. Occasionally you might quote a line or two, if they seem to especially capture the thought. But the point is to begin the transition to your own words, which is the transition to your own thoughts.

In the third stage, you will return to the Source Note and begin analyzing it, describing your reaction to the source material and how it relates to a problem you are working on or a question you're addressing. As you write a new note, which I call a Point Note, the focus shifts from the source material to *your own thoughts*. This is where you begin taking real ownership of the idea, using the source as support for a thought you're pursuing; a point you want to make.

Although it will vary widely depending on the content you're working with, the ratio of these types of notes will probably contract sharply as you move from highlights to source notes to points and make them your own. In some cases, the reduction to be in orders of magnitude: you might distill a hundred highlights into ten Source

Notes you want to preserve and one or two Points. This is a pretty good result, if after making note of a hundred items in a text that catch your attention you manage to achieve an important insight. And obviously, the more Source Notes you make, the more insights you can expect to gain.

So if the first step in creating new knowledge and then reporting on it is finding sources and learning from texts, the very first question of all might be, what is a text? For our purposes, a text can be any statement you run into in written, visual, or spoken form. One of the two epigrams at the beginning of this chapter came from a centuries-old book, the other quote is from a recent movie. Many scholars in specialized fields also consider images, artworks, or music to be texts they can analyze. At the very least, in the context of a class, anything you read in a textbook, an assigned reading, a primary source, or a lecture is a text. You can take notes on what the instructor says and review those notes later. Even a discussion can be a source of valuable notes, if people have prepared their arguments. All the material you're putting into the "mill", grinding up, analyzing, rearranging, thinking about, and turning into new knowledge, counts.

In today's world, we can reasonably expect that the need to continue learning will be life-long. So we should be constantly looking for new information to expand our understanding; thinking about texts and analyzing them all the time. An important element of this is critical thinking. Try not to passively accept what you're told or what you read. Ask questions, look for evidence that might corroborate or challenge claims, and compare what you're reading or hearing with things you've heard before, things you've read, things you believe. And write your thoughts down, because, again, *writing is thinking*. And to be effective, thinking should be written down. We've probably all experienced an "Aha!" moment, when out of the blue, things we've been pondering suddenly fit together and make sense. But how often have we lost that insight, because we failed to write it down and then forgot it. Also, trust me on this: the "Aha!" moments become more frequent and rewarding, when you're writing thoughts down.

Writing notes is really pretty easy, once you get the hang of it. And it's a way of proving to yourself (and eventually, to others) that you've understood the text. Our notes can also provide us some clues into what in a text actually interested us. Where a source's ideas really excite us, notes will cluster. Even so, we should try to write a separate note for each discrete idea. It's not that helpful to have a three-thousand-word review of a book you've just read, when you are looking for a particular point. I say this from experience! Getting in the habit of recording one idea per note makes the ideas easier to find, and trains us to write succinctly, in plain language. Single-idea notes are also easier to mix and match with other ideas they agree with, disagree with, or modify in interesting ways. This is useful, because by the time an idea has made it into a Point Note, it has been well-filtered by our interests and is ready to be compared with other ideas. Some of the questions you can use are:

- How is this new idea relevant to the question I'm considering?
- Is this idea similar to or different from the others to which I'm comparing it?
- Does it agree or disagree?
- Are there other connections that may not have

been mentioned in the source?

"Comparing notes" is a metaphor for talking through ideas for good reason. And it is often easier to compare ideas when we are looking at them on a page, rather than trying to work them out in our heads. Also, reviewing written notes helps us avoid several mental biases that can get in the way of understanding. A bias called the "Mere-exposure Effect" suggests that we often mistake familiarity for expertise. We also tend to prefer information we have seen more recently to information we learned a long time ago. Finally, because we seek confirmation, we often overlook inconsistencies and contradictions. Written notes can help illuminate these inconsistencies, as well as putting both "old" and "new" data on an equal footing. They can also remind us that we have changed over time, by providing a written reminder of what we thought in the past.

Sometimes the notes we make live in an in-between world where they are partly data and partly interpretation. This is okay. With practice, your Source Notes will become more like data and your Points more analytical. Sometimes this requires revisiting a note several times. I'm not a big fan of "spaced repetition", because I'm not always trying to keep an idea in my memory. But I do think that reviewing notes is important and should be a regular practice. Source Notes and especially Point Notes should be written in a way that you will understand them out of context, without having to reacquaint yourself with the entire train of thought; or another reader will understand them.

Finally, new notes should be connected with an existing note when you add them to your system. I'll describe this in greater detail shortly; the point for now is that linking a new thought to an existing train of thought seems to be a key to your note-making system working for you. Where does this new idea fit into your thoughts on an issue? Your questions about a topic? Your ideas about a puzzle you're working on understanding? Disciplining yourself to make this connection can be a bit tough and time-consuming at first. It is worth the investment. Without understanding how these ideas that interest us fit together, all we have is a pile of unrelated trivia.

Once you've discovered a text you're going to process for its ideas, analyzing the text is the same as analyzing any other mechanism. You take it apart so you can see what it's supposed to do and how it does its job. Author W.H. Auden demystified both literature and criticism when he said, "Here is a verbal contraption. How does it work?" In the next chapter, we'll dig deeper into the mechanics of making notes and working with ideas.

# 3

# WORKING WITH IDEAS

*The only true praise is thought. The only thing that can back-bone an essay is thought.* Robert Frost (1874-1963)

*Nobody ever starts from scratch.* Sönke Ahrens.

To set the scene and provide a bit of context, I'm going to briefly discuss some details of my personal note-making process. I want to say up front that this is *a possible* way of making notes, not the only way, because I think a lot of the way you approach any text depends on the reason you're looking at it in the first place. However, there are good reasons why I want to get to a specific endpoint: Point Notes I can use to further develop a train of thought that will lead to output.

So here's an example. Historian William Cronon's big

book is called *Nature's Metropolis: Chicago and the Great West*. Published in 1991, this has become a core text of environmental history that has influenced a generation of scholars. I first read the book in a graduate Environmental History class at the University of Massachusetts, and then I reread it for my comprehensive exams. Since then I've read *in the book* and I've assigned chapters to my students. But I haven't read the whole book cover to cover for a decade. It's probably time to do that again, and see what I think of it now and what ideas jump out at me today that the previous me passed by.

When I first read the book, I highlighted passages I thought were important, based on whatever I was interested in at the time. Some of the highlights were directed at understanding the author's argument and his main points, since that was my goal in the first cover-to-cover reading. I wrote a review of the book that discussed and critiqued Cronon's ideas and methods. Later, I went back looking for particular things such as Cronon's use of the Central Place theory, of which I was a bit critical. Or details of the growth of the Chicago industries he covers. These details became very important to me, when I was writing my own lectures and a textbook chapter covering these topics. I also mined his endnotes and the bibliography and added a lot of books to my reading list by looking at the things that had influenced Cronon's thinking on the topic. Later, I returned looking for specific details of the lumber industry as well as the way he tells the story, as I begin thinking about researching and writing more on this topic.

I had not paid extremely close attention to the lumber industry portions of the book in the past, but now that this has become a question I'm actively working on, I discovered new and important information from rereading. The point is that any good book like *Nature's Metropolis* includes a lot more information than you are probably going to capture in even a close reading. I think it's often an issue for people when they first become note-makers: an anxiety about getting the "right" stuff out of a book, or even "all the stuff". I don't think this is completely possible, and I think it's increasingly less possible, the better the book. I might even say the best books *are the best books* because they stubbornly defy being reduced to a synopsis and some notes. Another way of saying that is, great books have *so much* in them that many different people with many different interests can all find something they'll value in their pages.

So let's jettison the idea that we're ever going to be able to completely encompass a 250,000-word book in a note! When you think of it that way, it's a bit absurd, isn't it? What then is the point of taking notes? It is to enter a relationship with the ideas in a text; potentially one that will expand and deepen over time, as you return to the source with new questions. Not every book will be one you'll want to have this type of relationship with, of course. There are plenty of sources that only have a couple of things to tell you, to contribute to your project. Or one. Or none at all. That's mostly a function of your interests and questions. It's very rare that a book gets out there into the world that has nothing relevant to say to anybody, but your interests may be specific enough that it may have nothing in it you need to know.

When I reread the book again, cover to cover, I might grab a different color highlighter. I'll try not to be too influenced by my previous highlights, although from time to time I imagine I'll stop and ask myself why I focused on some lines on a page and not others. There's an often-repeated claim that Niklas Luhmann rarely returned to texts after once reading them. I suspect he was often looking for particular information when he read an article or a book; I don't think that having a note-taking system means you will always get everything you need from a text on the first pass through it. If you're a student and a text has been assigned in a class, there may be a limit to the depth you want to dive into it or the time you want to spend. There may only be some specific questions you're seeking to answer. Once again, it's the purpose of picking up the book that determines how you process it.

Neuroscientists have shown that the human mind functions more effectively with (some even say, relies on) what they call "external scaffolding". Our attention and memory are both limited and are filtered by what seems urgent at the moment. This was originally a survival skill, but it is not always helpful, when we're trying to develop a complicated train of thought over the long term. And there's a type of stress called ego depletion that can seem like psychic muscle fatigue, which we can feel when we have big, unresolved problems or questions hanging over our heads. It's very helpful to have a system that we can trust, where we can break down a project into small, doable chunks and feel confident they aren't going to fall through the cracks. Just about any project can be broken into small, doable chunks.

Breaking a big project into pieces is important. "Getting Things Done" expert David Allen says it's impossible to work on a Project; you can only work on tasks that are part of a project. This is a valuable insight that can reduce a lot of anxiety. When I planned my PhD dissertation, I thought of the 300 pages I was going to have to write as about 500 paragraphs. I was relieved, because paragraphs are easy! All I needed was a place to store and organize my notes from all the primary and secondary sources I had accumulated, and line them up with the argument I was making about American History. Somewhere I could trust that they would be safe and I'd be able to find them when I needed them.

The system you use to make and store notes can be digital or physical. I've been playing with different apps for over a decade. The ones I used for my dissertation worked, but I've tried many new tools since then. Lately, I've returned to paper notes and a card catalog. The key, I think, is that you should be able to move your notes around, compare them with each other, try different combinations and orders to see if they help – and then return to where you were without losing valuable information. Paper note cards have all these flexibilities, so I'd suggest beginning with them and then letting your system evolve.

> *Quote — 31.63/2*
>
> *Ahrens: "Nobody ever starts from scratch."*
>
> *This is true both in the sense of standing on shoulders, and that a lot of pre-work has taken place when we sit down with a blank sheet or*

Because highlighting usually happens in the text you are

consuming, the first notes you'll probably write on a card will be Source Notes. These will be a combination of notable ideas from the source and the beginning of your take on them. For example, this was a card I wrote preparing for this project. It is one of those rare times when I actually quoted the source rather than paraphrasing, because I thought it was a powerful statement. It includes the thought I wanted to preserve from the text as well as my reaction to it. As I continue working with my thoughts about how to describe ideas and note-making, I will very rarely rely on quotes, although I have been using a few as epigrams at the beginnings of these chapters (never say never!). More often and more likely, I'll reformulate ideas into my own words, often even devising new metaphors to describe them. For example, months ago I read an article by Niklas Luhmann in which he said that notes in his file system not well connected by cross-references to other notes tended to never be seen again. They just got lost in the box forever. Over time, this resonated with other things I had been reading about the migrations of prehistoric peoples, from a book on paleogenetics. The result was this next card.

> **Connection**　　　　　　2.1.23/1
>
> The isolated factoid is like a prehistoric human cut off from the tribe. She's unlikely to survive or reproduce.

The idea of making these notes is described on these two cards. First, we never have to start from scratch. We don't need to discover fire, invent language, and organize a society in order to survive. Similarly, we usually don't need to return all the way to first principles to add to knowledge and contribute insights. What we *do need to do* is situate our work in a context that allows someone else to understand how our ideas connect to other knowledge. The way we do that is by keeping track of (and documenting clearly) where the ideas we are working with came from. Within our own notes, connections allow the ideas we are developing to survive by interacting with other ideas and remaining part of our train of thought.

The first of these example notes is a Source Note; the second is a Point Note. They both have keywords ("Quote" and "Connection"), the first being a bit vaguer and really less helpful in the long run than the second. A more specific keyword from a Point Note I derive from this card might be "Beginnings", if I decided to elaborate this idea as a comment on starting a project. Or I might use this source to contribute to another train of thought.

In the second case, checking "Connection" in my Index would lead me to this card. I might then compare this thought to others that use the same keyword, to see how it supports or modifies the idea of connection.

You may have noticed that on both of these cards I changed the number, as I improved my system. Rather than rewrite the cards to hide the change, I just replaced the old number with the new. These things happen, occasionally, as you evolve your system. I'll explain the numbering system in more detail later. Note also that the things that I'm saying about these ideas are completely subjective. They may be valuable or worthless, depending on how well I've thought things through. Like the things that jumped out at me from a text that I decided to highlight and make a Source Note from, my conclusions are my own and are based on my own interests and train of thought. There really isn't any right or wrong answer regarding what you should pursue, other than what interests you and your audience. If you are way off course and making no sense at all, your readers will let you know. Even if that reader is just future-you – and this is one of the benefits of making notes your future self can read!

The basic truth behind this idea of transferring ownership of ideas from our sources to ourselves is that we don't really own ideas at all. This is not to say that ideas exist independently of the people who think them, in some Platonic world of forms. But it IS to say that it's extremely rare to have a completely original thought that *no one* has ever had before. There are about seven billion people on the planet today and since the advent of *Homo sapiens* an estimated 107 billion people have lived. We learned language as babies, and we absorbed most of what we know about the world from our parents and the people we knew as children. Later we went to schools, read books, and watched screens. We didn't discover much on our own.

Even if we limit the discussion to the types of knowledge we acquire in school, we're still standing on the shoulders of others about 99.9% of the time. In many cases we work with these ideas with little thought of their sources. We may call an idea by a name, like the Pythagorean Theorem, but we don't worry that much about thanking Pythagoras — which is probably just as well, since the same idea is mentioned in the Baudhayana *Sulba-sutra* from India, which was written centuries before Pythagoras lived. But we do try to be careful with more recent ideas, especially in an academic setting.

Even though we give credit to authors by citing them in footnotes and including them in bibliographies, at its heart the learning process is very much about taking the thoughts of others and making them our own. We collect the ideas that interest us, connect them to other ideas that interest us, and then use them in ways that sometimes create new ideas or things. That may be by using what we know about right triangles to build a stable structure, or it might be by using ideas we discovered in texts to write something "original".

But what does the word original mean, if we've just admitted that we very rarely have a new thought no one has ever had before? A practical definition might include the fact that we have *done the work* of thinking through a problem and arriving at a solution. We've asked ourselves a question (or responded to someone else's question) with a train of thought that combines elements of information and interpretations we have accumulated, arranged in a way that seems to answer the question (or at least, provides insight into the problem). Some answers may be extremely straightforward, requiring us only to apply data readily at hand. Others may need combinations of ideas from a variety of sources, brought together and interpreted in creative and innovative ways.

Since the interesting and rewarding questions are usually the ones that call for these creative solutions drawing on ideas that may seem hard to imagine combining (until someone does, and then it's "so obvious"), the better we can become at collecting, understanding, and remembering information, the more likely we are to solve hard problems. The name of the game, then, is mastering the process of grabbing as much information as we can get our hands on, and making it our own. We do this by gradually transferring ownership of these ideas from the authors we read to ourselves by understanding the gist of an idea, paraphrasing it in our own words, and linking (comparing, contrasting) it to other ideas that interest us. These tasks prove (to ourselves and others) that we really understand the idea and make it possible for us to use it when we need it.

# 4

# HIGHLIGHTING AND TAKING NOTES

> *Everyone mines every book for the things that are useful to him, especially [books that are] rich and complex.* (Italo Calvino, 1923-1985)
>
> *I wanted to live deep and suck out all the marrow of life...* (Henry David Thoreau, 1817-1862).

You'll notice that in the chapter title, I use the words "Taking Notes" rather than what I typically say, *Making Notes*. This is not accidental. There is something we do that it seems appropriate to call note-taking. This is what we do when we write down what a lecturer is saying in a class, or a speaker in a meeting. Or when we jot down a couple of ideas we want to remember from a podcast or video or article. These are notes and ideas we've *taken from another source.* When we make our own Source and Point notes, we are beginning to form ideas of our own. So it's appropriate to call this first stage of just jotting something down note-taking — but then let's give ourselves credit as makers.

Both of the quotes above are basically talking about the same thing. Everything we read and everything we experience is valuable material for our minds. You may have heard pundits say in recent years America has shifted from being primarily busy making things and has become an information economy. More Americans than ever before have become "knowledge workers". What we're talking about here, thinking about texts or experiences and turning them into insights, definitely qualifies as knowledge work.

Let's examine these quotes a bit more closely. Calvino uses the metaphor of mining, suggesting that we dig beneath the surface of things, to find the iron ore that will become steel girders supporting our structures of interpretation. And Thoreau — can you believe he only lived to be 45? He wanted to suck the marrow out of life, like a hunter-gatherer intent on getting all the nutrition out of his prey. Or like a modern-day chef, who roasts and breaks large bones and then boils them for stock because that's where the flavor is.

These are useful metaphors. We can imagine mining the information we encounter, following veins and seams underground, then smelting and refining the ore into useful metals. Occasionally we might come across gems that are nearly perfect when we discover them, perhaps needing only a bit of cutting and setting to reveal their beauty. But mostly the work involves patience and effort, as we go through the steps of finding, collecting, refining, and concentrating information from a raw material into exactly what we need for our structure. Or, we can picture ourselves collecting bones, breaking and roasting them, and then boiling them for hours or days in a stock pot to release the nutritious and tasty marrow.

In both metaphors, the process takes time and effort. This is also accurate. You've no doubt heard the saying attributed to Thomas Edison, that "Genius is 1% inspiration and 99% perspiration." Whether or not he was correct about the proportion, Edison's point was a good one. People sometimes imagine that working with ideas is essentially different from other types of work; that knowledge workers are a special elite group (or believe themselves to be). In fact, working with ideas is just like any other type of work. It can be very exciting at times! It can often also be very routine and repetitive. But much of the value and most of the inspiration (whether it's 1% or 10% or more) comes directly from that less exciting, more work-like part.

When we're working with ideas, the information we are processing is just a basic raw material. We apply techniques and use tools to turn this raw material into something useful and valuable to our purpose. The techniques and tools we're going to discuss in this section on note-making are focused mostly on texts, but they can be applied to ideas that come to you from discussion, listening to lectures, experiment, or life experience.

The first step in creating new knowledge and reporting on it, is finding sources and learning from texts. As I've mentioned, there are several ways to approach a text, depending on what you are hoping to get from it. First, you might find yourself assigned to read something you know nothing about. Second, you might choose to read a text because it has been recommended or cited by someone else. Third, you might be reading with a specific question in mind. We will discuss the details of these reading process as we continue this section. For now, a few observations:

1. The way you are going to engage with a text depends on what you are hoping to learn from it. If you are looking for a particular piece of data to answer a specific question, then you are probably going to read much more quickly and with that goal in mind. This is what Calvino was saying above, about everyone mining the book for what's useful to them. If it's a large text, you may be searching for a needle in a haystack. You won't be paying much attention to each individual stalk of straw, since you'll be focused on finding your needle.
2. This type of hyper-focus is a lot different from the type of openness to the author's intentions that you might want to try to practice, if you were reading a novel for a literature class. Although it is probably impossible for readers to make themselves into completely "blank slates", bringing absolutely no expectations or preconceptions to a text, there are times when it is helpful to try to be as open to surprise as possible and let an author tell their story or make their argument or offer their interpretation without prejudgment.
3. I am not implying that openness is something you need more with literature and focus should

be reserved for non-fiction. There will be times in both genres when it will be appropriate to approach a text with a specific question in mind, and other times when a better strategy will be to let the text surprise you.

We read different texts for different reasons, regardless of the subject. It's probably useful to know, however, that when we are hyper-focused and looking for that needle of data, we may be missing something else that might be valuable in the haystack. That's not necessarily a problem — we're usually not planning to burn the haystack after we find the needle. We can always return to see what else the author might have had to say about other topics. Some of them might be adjacent to the needle topic, others could take us in entirely different directions.

This is one of the cool things about engaging with other people's ideas: often their interests are just a little different from ours, and can take us in directions we may not have anticipated. We'll explore this idea more as we dig into some of the techniques and tools of note-taking in the rest of this section.

By now you've probably learned in an English class how authors use plot, imagery, symbolism, and allusion to express ideas and values in literature. We often forget that authors of nonfiction do this too, using pretty much the same set of language tools. This is how reporters write the news and historians tell stories. Even physicists, when they leave equations behind and try to describe their discoveries to the rest of us in plain English, find themselves employing analogies, metaphors, and the other language tools we all use. Writing an interpretive essay uses these same language tools, so as you're learning to recognize how different authors do it, remember that you're going to be doing it too.

When you take notes on a lecture or a video, you're beginning the writing process. Yes, if it's for a class you're recording *information* that might be on the exam. But you are also hearing an argument – the speaker isn't just reciting some random set of facts off the top of her head. Most lectures are built around a central question or idea. If the lecturer doesn't come right out and tell you what that is (clue: does the syllabus have lecture titles? Are they in the form of questions?), try to figure it out. If it doesn't come to you in class, review your notes later and try to boil the lecture's theme down to a sentence or two. If you're really stumped, ask.

You'll want to take notes when you read, too. You've already learned how most writers work: how they *generally* organize arguments, how they *generally* use setting and point of view to create atmosphere and mood; how they *generally* present narrators and characters to engage problems, etc. These are valuable clues to help you begin determining what a text might "mean" – *in general*. Your task is to analyze them in the *specific* context of the particular text you are reading and interpret how they make *that contraption* work. You might find once you get used to it, that such active reading doesn't diminish, but actually increases the pleasure you get from the text.

As you read or listen, your highlights or rough notes should explore both the "facts" in the text (who did what, when, where, how, and, if indicated, why?) and what the facts might suggest. But don't be too surprised if "facts" and "interpretations" are sometimes difficult to distinguish. And there's a reason why we discuss these texts in groups, rather than each pondering them on our own. We're all looking for the "truth" of our subject, whether it is a non-fiction article or a novel. As Franz Kafka noted in his diary, "one person cannot express the truth, but a host of perspectives might come close to this goal."

I usually tell my students that discussions go more smoothly and productively if they have already read the assignment and begun a dialogue with the text *before* they come to class. That used to mean underlining or highlighting interesting passages and writing a few questions and comments in the margins of a book. More recently I've discovered that more *active* measures such as writing down their thoughts after reading help students remember much more than just highlighting. The effort involved in writing a note in their own words, which instructional designers like to call a "desirable difficulty" helps shift the idea from short-term to long-term memory (this is the same reason many note-makers are shifting back to hand-writing on cards rather than depending on automated apps). I've found that if students have written some notes and thoughts about a reading, they arrive in class as an active member of an exploratory party and not as a passive fellow traveler, just along for the ride.

So how much and what should you highlight, when you begin to work with a text? How much can vary widely, based on what and why you are reading. Generally, though, it's a good rule of thumb to shoot for orders of magnitude. Try to highlight at most about ten percent of a text. Then try to write ten Source Notes based on each hundred of the most interesting highlights. Then try to write just one or two Point Notes for each ten Source Notes.

But *what* should you be highlighting? Begin with anything at all that you're not sure about, that you don't understand, that you'd like explained. Start with basic questions that clarify facts, then move on to interpretations. Compare the reading with other readings you've done, or with lecture and discussion notes. Add questions that reflect your interests and concerns – they're usually the issues that lead to good discussions and essays.

Here are some questions you might want to answer for yourself as you read, divided between fiction and nonfiction. Use what fits:

For Fiction (mostly)

- If it's a narrative, who is telling the story? Is the narrator reliable? Unreliable? Biased? Recognizing the narrator's point of view will help you evaluate the "facts" of the story.
- What is the setting and tone? What are you allowed to see, hear, taste, touch, smell, and feel – both physically and emotionally? Is there a sense of comedy, tragedy, irony?
- Who are the major and minor characters? What are their concerns? What motivates them? Who are you supposed to identify with?
- What kind of language is being used? What level of diction? What might that indicate?
- How is the plot structured? How are the issues and problems organized? Are there challenges and responses? Is there a recognizable archetype (hero's journey, classical tragedy, etc.)?
- What images and motifs recur? What kinds of terms, images, patterns are repeated? Can you

recognize metaphors? To what do they point?
- How does it end? What is resolved? What is the significance of the ending? Why does it end where it does?

For Non-fiction (mostly)

- Who is the author? What is the author's background? Is the author qualified to be the authority on the material in the piece?
- Who is the original audience for the text? How does the author feel about the audience? Are they allies? Opponents? Neutral readers the author is trying to convince of something?
- What is the author's intention? Is the text explanatory? Polemical? Celebratory? Why was it written?
- How is the argument structured? Does the author appeal to logic or emotion? What type of argument does the author use?

Fiction and non-fiction texts are generally built around narrative and argument (although, often, narrative can be a sneaky form of argument). Most readers are familiar with the basic forms of arguments described by Aristotle (384-322 BCE), the student of Plato and teacher of Alexander the Great. Aristotle recognized logical syllogisms as the most powerful types of arguments. A series of agreed-upon premises leads to an irrefutable conclusion.

Unfortunately, most of the time we don't have the advantage of being able to argue from premises that are incontrovertible facts. Sometimes an author's job is to show her readers new facts in order to lead them to a conclusion. Other times, what we're really arguing about is the truth of our premises. We live in a world of uncertainty, after all. So many of our arguments are based on premises that are tentative, leading to probable rather than absolute conclusions. Sometimes authors go to great lengths to *pretend* their premises are sound and their conclusions irrefutable. It's our job as readers to come to our own conclusions.

This may all seem ridiculously abstract. We don't spend much time these days, taking apart the way we think and looking at the parts. But when a political leader makes a claim such as "Markets should be unregulated," or "We hold these truths to be self-evident, that all men are created equal", there's a trail of argument supporting that statement. If you want to understand (or challenge) the claim, the best place to look is at the premises that lead to that conclusion.

The form of argument we've been discussing is called deduction. It builds from accepted facts to a specific conclusion. There are two other forms authors use frequently. Induction goes more or less in the opposite direction, starting with observations or evidence (like data in a scientific experiment) and ending with a general conclusion. Since in the real world we never have a chance to look at *all* the data, these conclusions are always, by definition, tentative. But in life we often take inductive ideas as facts. We know what's going to happen when we throw a ball, not because we've studied physics and calculus, but because we've done it before and experienced the results. Even so, careful scientists still talk about the *theory* of evolution. They don't do this because scientists aren't convinced that evolution is correct, but because there's always the possibility that new evidence will be found that will require them to adjust the theory. The point is, inductive reasoning is supposed to follow where the data leads it.

Aristotle actually identified a third form of argument that may surprise you: narrative. Historian Hayden White defined history as a verbal artifact that we use to "combine a certain amount of data, theoretical concepts for explaining these data, and a narrative structure for their presentation." Stories and anecdotes persuade us because we *identify* with the people and situations described. A good story can even sometimes take the place of data (induction) or even agreed-on facts (deduction) in an argument. The most powerful stories can reach past the logical appeal to reason, bringing the emotions of the audience into play. Fear, pride, contentment, resentment, love, and moral outrage are all powerful elements of argument, so it's important to be able to recognize whether a writer is appealing to reason or to emotion. And then to ask why.

# 5

# MAKING SOURCE NOTES

> *You should read with a pen in your hand and enter...short hints of what you feel...may be useful; for this be the best method of imprinting [them] in your memory.* Benjamin Franklin (1706-1790)

> *To be able to play with ideas, we first have to liberate them from their original context by means of abstraction and respecification.* Sönke Ahrens.

As I mentioned previously, sometimes people feel a sense of "writer's block" at the beginning of a new project, but often that feeling comes from a misunderstanding. In his book *How to Take Smart Notes*, Sönke Ahrens criticizes writing teachers who encourage their students to "brainstorm" to come up with a topic for an essay or a research project. I think processes that include free association and a sense of informal openness to surprising combinations of ideas can be very useful, especially in group settings. However, I tend to agree with Ahrens that if I've already done the work of highlighting, making Source Notes, and then turning them into Point Notes, then coming up with a topic to write about ought to be the least of my concerns. The whole point of this note-making process is not only to provide ourselves with ideas we want to pursue, but to actually *show us* which ideas we are most interested in. We'll see this process in action as we continue. Right now, let's look a the first stage in the writing process: reviewing highlights and turning the best ideas we found into Source Notes.

Boiling important ideas we encounter down into a sentence or two is the key skill we learn in this process. Taking a complex narrative from literature, or a textbook chapter, or a primary source, or a lecture and being able to say, "This is what that was about" is a crucial step in the journey from hearing about the knowledge of others to creating our own.

Highlighting is something most of us have been doing for so long that it may seem obvious. But you may have noticed a difference between the way you may have been taught to interact with texts and the suggestions you have found here. This difference mostly revolves around a slight redefinition of our relationship with texts. Although some texts you may read may be pillars of their disciplines, or even of a wider community or culture, in the note-making we are practicing here, the point is not so much appreciation as information. We are not reading texts simply to experience their greatness, but to learn something. Often something quite specific, that answers a particular question we are pursuing. While it's still possible to maintain an attitude of reverence for a particular text or for great writing in general, it's sometimes helpful to tone down that emotion a bit when we approach texts to learn from them — especially if that feeling makes it more difficult to read with a critical eye.

Once we have read and highlighted, the next step is to go back and review the highlighted passages. Rather than just copying down a quotation of what the author said, we try to summarize it in our own words. This is the stage when I begin to paraphrase rather than quote, unless there's a really compelling reason to quote. Paraphrasing is how I demonstrate (to myself, at this point) that I got the author's point. It is also the beginning of my response: what I write down and how I describe it helps me nail down my interpretation of the author's point. It's the beginning of a conversation between me as the reader, the text's author, and my ultimate reader.

Summarizing and Paraphrasing are very closely related in this process. Educational research has shown that when students restate something they have learned in their own words, the information is much likelier to move from their short-term to long-term memories. This is probably because the words or images they use to describe the new knowledge already have a home in their world-view. Connecting them to an existing idea in their understanding of the world seems to create places for the new ideas to occupy in the students' memories.

For an academic perspective, consider Luhmann's description (quoted in Ahrens' book):

> The best method is to take notes — not excerpts, but condensed, reformulated accounts of a text. Rewriting what was already written almost

> automatically trains one to shift the attention towards frames, categories, and patterns ...conditions and assumptions.

Working in the style of Luhmann, we could use the note to comment on the structure of the author's argument or her assumptions, as well as simply summarizing her findings.

Some people might be concerned that as we paraphrase what an author wrote, we run the risk of changing their original meaning. This is probably true, but it is rarely something we ought to worry about. Even *quoting* changes the original meaning of a passage, since it removes the words from their original context in the text. Quoting or paraphrasing passages selectively or out of context has certainly been used to subvert the meanings of texts throughout history. But, I would argue, rarely by accident.

Paraphrasing is no more suspect than quoting, as far as accurately reflecting a text goes. But the added value of paraphrasing is that we are frequently not pursuing the same question as the author whose writing we are making into notes. We may have found a piece of data or an argument that is relevant to our pursuit in a completely different way than it functioned in the text where we found it. Or, like Luhmann, we may be interested in deconstructing the text's frames, categories, etc.

Another objection people have raised about paraphrasing is that it is a short step from plagiarism, or at least on a slippery slope on the way to it. This is another misunderstanding. We have already seen how nearly all the knowledge we have is inherited from others. We use countless pieces of what we call "general knowledge" every minute without citing the sources where we first encountered them (if we can even remember them!). But the type of knowledge we're taking from sources and making our own in our notes is a bit more specific than this general knowledge. Its sources deserve to be cited, because they are often recent and identifiable. And they *need to be* cited, because the sources provide a context for our own ideas without which they would lose a lot of their meaning and value.

> Students/Motivation ?????
> 2.1.1.1/21
> Ahrens says Luhmann never forced himself to work on anything he did not enjoy, but was nonetheless super productive. Or maybe that's why.
>
> (Ahrens 5)

So it is a regular part of note-making that we have a bibliography attached to our system of notes, where we store a complete record of the sources we have engaged with. When we write a source note, we cite the source just as if we were placing a footnote in an article. Later, if we use the note in an article, the citation can become a footnote.

You'll notice that in addition to the citation, this Source Note contains keywords. These are like tags in an online system; they describe the idea on the card, even if the keyword is not mentioned in the idea. Neither "students" nor "motivation" is mentioned on the card, but that is the context I chose for the idea, when I was thinking about where in my outline for this book it ought to go. As it turns out, I used this idea early in Chapter 1. I know this because of the card number on the top right, which corresponds to the last section of that chapter (the numerical range of the notes I used was 3.1.1.1/1 to 3.1.1.1/25).

This brings us to the often misunderstood and sometimes controversial issue of note numbering. The difference between many digital systems and paper is that when we use a physical note system we have to write an Index Note and keep track the address of this note somehow, so we can find it later. Each note is going to be filed in a drawer in a card catalog. But not randomly. It will be filed by its card number.

This is not *necessarily* the case in digital note-making systems. It is possible to enter a note in a word processing app or a notes app such as Obsidian without tagging it any way. Nearly all software today includes powerful search capabilities. For that matter, operating systems include tools such as Spotlight Search that will allow you to find files that include keywords you can remember. But what if the idea you want to associate a note with does not appear in the text of your note? You've already seen a couple of examples of my notes where this is the case.

In a digital system, keywords and tags are probably a minimal level of identification for your notes. Writing something down does you very little good, beyond helping to cement a thought in your long-term memory, if you can't find the note when you need it. I have experienced the frustration that comes from knowing I have long ago written about a source or an idea that would be very useful to a problem I'm working on, but not being able to locate it. I have multi-terabyte external storage that I can query with nearly-instant full-text searches. There are still times when I can't find what I'm looking for. Even my more recent note system, in a brand-new, purpose-built app, became a "black hole" of thousands of notes that I could *not easily search and arrange*. This was not the fault of the app. The problem was that I had not left myself a bread-crumb trail that would lead me back to the ideas I had entered, or show me how they were connected to other ideas I was already working with, in the system.

Luckily, this is not an impossible situation to rectify. I am gradually reviewing my big mountain of notes, chipping off individual rocks and pebbles; connecting some and throwing others away. It's a time-consuming process and seems especially wasteful because I'm discarding notes I don't think I need. I can't help wondering how much farther ahead I might be if I had chosen the right notes and connected them as I made them, in real-time?

The error I made, that I want to warn you against, is sometimes called the "collector's fallacy". Having a well-stocked library is great. But it is not the same as making a system of notes that capture and elaborate your ideas. And the distance between a personal knowledge management app filled with clippings and highlights that I haven't thought about is about as great, I've found, as if I had just highlighted a book and put it back on the shelf. It's better than nothing. But not what I was hoping for. Not what the PKM gurus promised, and I imagine not what you are looking for if you have bothered to read this far.

> *Keywords*          *Hare*
>                                       *3.1.2.2/k*
>
> *An index (paper or dig.) can create a list of keywords that can be the place where concentrations appear.*
>
> *tag?*

There are two levels of identifying each and every thought you put into your system, that I urge you to use. The first is tagging each note with a keyword that identifies what the idea described in the note is *about*. The keywords should reflect topics that are of interest to you, rather than a predetermined list of categories like the Library of Congress catalog system. The note-cards that are contributing to this section of the chapter use the tag "Keywords". This card, for example, describes the index that can show us where clusters of interest are concentrating. While it is valuable to have the keyword on the card as you're shuffling through a small deck of them to arrange your thoughts, it is indispensable once you have more notes than you can spread across a big table and sort at once.

An Index is something you must physically create as you add cards in a physical note system. You create an alphabetized list, where you make a quick entry for each new note, under its keyword. This is where the card's unique number shows its value. The Index card becomes a list of card numbers that can direct you to ideas throughout your system and show you connections between different trains of thought.

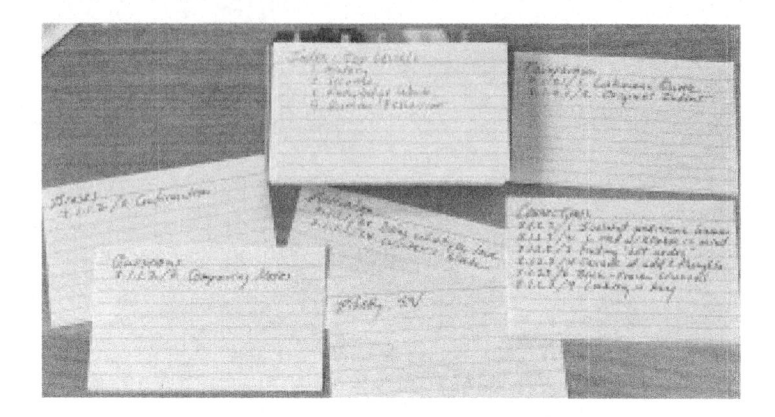

But why not just create a category called "Keywords" and file every card you write on that topic in that section? This might be all you need, if your notes are directed toward a small, immediate goal. If you are writing a research paper, for example, and you're planning on throwing the notes away when you are done, then it may make sense to stick with just keywords. But what if the question or project you are working on is bigger? What if you are researching for a thesis, or studying for your profession, or pursuing a lifelong interest? Then you will probably find that ideas related to a particular "keyword" thought can come from different sources at different times. And, even more important, many ideas can be relevant to more than one train of thought. Often, the exciting, innovative ideas you'll come up with will be interdisciplinary, or at least will involve combinations of ideas you encountered in different contexts.

This is not to say that you should put a half-dozen keywords on every card. Most will have one; a few will get a couple right away. Some will get another keyword later, when you have revisited the idea and considered it from a new angle. The unique card number is also incredibly valuable when you want to create a link between a new thought you are adding to the system and one particular other thought, rather than a category of thoughts. Another of the practices that is crucial to making useful, connected notes is identifying a specific note to file each new note "behind" in the numerical sequence. We'll cover that in detail shortly; for now it's enough to understand that each idea is a unique thought in the note system, and gets its own card, keyword, and number.

Numbering systems have also been a source of controversy in the PKM community. Some users of digital systems eschew numbers entirely, believing that the searchability of the system and the ability to create "Maps of Content" make numbering redundant and pointless. As someone who has seen my digital system become a mushy mess of hard-to-locate ideas, I disagree. Also, I have seen my ideas about how to organize my "Map" change over time; requiring time-consuming reorganization of my notes. Finally, although I had noticed clusters forming and had been able to see connections in "graph views" of my data, I was not satisfied with my ability to *get information out* of the digital system. It satisfied the "collector" in me, but not so much the writer.

The numbers themselves have also been a source of debate. Some digital users identify a new note chronologically. One I made right now, for example, might be numbered "202207201003", which would be unique in my system, provided I don't make another this minute. The advantage of this system is that I could keep track of when I had particular ideas, which might come in handy sometime in the future. The disadvantage is that the number doesn't convey any additional information, and it doesn't allow me to choose where to insert a new note "behind" the existing note it is most closely related to.

I'm going to briefly describe how I am currently numbering my notes. I *do not* claim that this is the only way that works, or that it's the best system for you. I don't even claim that it's the system I'm going to stick with forever. But it works for me and you're welcome to use it as a starting point, and then tweak it for your own needs as you become more familiar with your own unique process.

Developing a numbering scheme, I wanted to remain focused on *getting to output*, rather than trying to conform to any standards of correct taxonomy. For example, I don't think it's wrong just to begin numbering the first card "1" and the second one "2" and just carry on from there. The keywords and index are really the most important things here, to allow you to find and link your thoughts. Ultimately, the number of a card is not meaningful, except as a unique identity and as a way to locate it. So it would be perfectly okay to begin with "1" and "2", and then when you have another thought that modifies "1", put it behind that card and call it "1a".

My own numbering system began as a reaction to a conversation with another analog note user who recommended using a top-level numbering scheme that classifies knowledge by disciplines. Another friend suggested that if we were going to begin creating a shared space where others could view our notes on the web and if everyone used a common system that had the same number for the same discipline, it might be helpful. I think both ideas have merit, but I decided not to base my private notes on standardized categories. I don't want to create a bunch of empty "folders" I may never fill, and I prefer my "trees" of knowledge to grow organically and not be tied to a predetermined "trellis".

So my numbering system has a couple of peculiarities. Firstly, it has two number series, separated by a divider. For example, 1.4.2.15/16a. The numbers on the left of the divider are nested categories, like folders. The number to the right belongs to the actual card that corresponds with a single idea. The idea may be a piece of evidence or an argument; that is, a Source Note or a Point Note. So the overall number tells me something about how the idea is related to other ideas (the nested "folders") as well as where it fits in a conversation with other ideas (the sequence number and letter).

Rather than choosing a set of top-level domains that reflected disciplines or the Library of Congress or the Dewey Decimal system, I chose the three things I thought I would be making notes on, History, Science, and Knowledge Work. Later I added a fourth, Human Behavior. I numbered them 1 to 4. History is "1". Within History, I made seven additional categories for the six continents and one for "World". I started with Africa, because that's where humans began. Within the fourth subdivision, which was North America, I used "1" for my Secular Radicals project and "2" for my Primary Source project. So now I have a Topic, "History of North American Secular Radicals" that has a number 1.4.1. Primary Sources are 1.4.2. In that topic I have fifteen "folders" for the fifteen weeks of my semester. In some of these topics I have dozens of files. None of this was pre-planned as I was setting up the system. I added the branches as I needed them.

So 1.4.2.15/16a means: 1: History, 4: North America, 2: Primary Sources, 15: Reconstruction, /16: Politics in the South, a: An additional thought I had about this source. The additional thought I had in the "a" note is the beginning of an argument I want to make about Southern politics during Reconstruction. This is a "Point Note", where note 1.4.2.15/16 was more of a "Source Note" (although it had a bit of interpretation on it, too). This is an example of how I'm not particularly interested in what the note is called; what matters is how it contributes to building the output I'm working on (in this case a Primary Source reader for my US History course).

The two main ways I will be able to access the idea on this note are first, that it will be physically present in the card drawer, so when I go there looking for my primary sources about the Reconstruction period of American History, it will be right where I need it. The second way I could find it would be if I was looking specifically for notes on Southern Politics, I could find it in the Index by searching "Politics" or "American South". On each of those Index cards it would be surrounded by other entries on those topics that might create meaningful new contexts for the ideas in the note.

A new note in an existing series is typically added at the end. But when we return to a particular thought in that series and decide we want to add a comment on that particular note, we can do that by "branching" with a letter. For example, if I returned to note 3.1.2.2/2 (the note on keywords in the photo above) in the future and had an additional thought I wanted to record to modify the idea, I could add a note 3.1.2.2/2a and insert it in front of 3.1.2.2/3. If I return again and want to modify 3.1.2.2/2a, I can alternate back to a number (3.1.2.2/2a1). If I have *another* new thought about 3.1.2.2/2, I can call that 3.1.2.2/2b. The point of this elaborate numbering is that I can have a conversation with myself regarding this train of thought, over time. Like a real conversation, each new statement doesn't invalidate or erase the previous ones, but builds on them. Our ideas evolve over time, and even moreso when we are aware of and participate in that evolution.

# 6

# DISCOVERING TOPICS AND CONNECTIONS

> *Every note is just an element in the network of references and back-references in the system, from which it gains its utility.* Niklas Luhmann (1927-1998)

> *It's so much easier to see what worked than to predict what might work.* Sönke Ahrens

In this chapter, we will look at the practical issues involved in choosing a topic and the ways we can connect ideas and create Point Notes. To begin with the practical: if you are a student, there's a degree of arbitrariness involved in your note-making that probably does not apply to independent scholars pursuing their own interests. For example, the texts you'll need to work with, early in your education, are probably givens. In English they are often the "classics," books that a consensus of informed readers have identified as the most significant of their times. In History we also have texts (primary and secondary) that are foundational to our understanding of an event or a period.

The process of becoming a classic or a core text in a discipline is interesting and involves both the innumerable readings the texts have undergone and the ongoing construction of our common culture. But that's not really the point we're exploring here. The particular texts you might be responsible for understanding in a given class were chosen out of a universe of possible texts because they fit together and because, as a group, they lead somewhere. When you figure out how they fit together and where they lead, you'll be well on your way to understanding the overall theme of the course or discipline – which, remember, is also a text!

Because my father (who wrote the first version of this handbook) taught surveys on the foundational literature of Euro-American culture and I am a historian, at the risk of sounding like an old fart I'll say just one more thing about "classics." Whether we respond positively or negatively to the works themselves, or to what's included and excluded from the list, it's difficult to ignore their influence. When we off-handedly characterize something as being "Quixotic" or "Kafkaesque"; when our newspapers and popular magazines talk about "Progressives" or the "Frontier"; when political cartoons, hip-hop music, and even Sunday comics depend on our familiarity with Beowulf and Odysseus and Malcolm X and Viet Nam in order to get their points, then we would be wise to become familiar with these concepts, characters, and events.

In any case, whatever their source, as we're educating ourselves we engage with texts: a set of assigned readings, lectures, discussions, books, articles, videos, podcasts, archives, etc. Let's think of them as a challenge. How are we going to make these texts meaningful to ourselves? *This is a basic question in life.* Every day we deal with things not under our control. The poet Robert Frost once claimed that every one of his poems was "one of these adaptations that I've made. I've taken whatever you give me and made it what I want it to be." We've already begun responding to this challenge by taking notes on what we have read and heard. Even if a discussion and essay assignment in a class is very directed – "Discuss the relationship between Quixote and Sancho Panza in *Don Quixote*" or "Compare John Muir's attitude toward wilderness with Gifford Pinchot's based on their writing about the Hetch Hetchy controversy" – there's nearly always a way to make an aspect of the topic your own.

If, on the other hand, you have a chance to discover your own topic, you're faced with a different challenge – but that's still no reason for panic or "writer's block,". You've already begun the process. Your notes are written thoughts, and they are the source of what you'll contribute to a discussion or write. Passages you marked in your text or notes you wrote in your notebook have already begun becoming your own thoughts as you turned them into Source Notes. These represent the main facts and ideas you were looking for, and record your personal reactions to what interested you in the text. That's why everybody's notes are a little different. When you think about and expand upon these personal reactions, you'll discover the beginnings of your individual interpretation of the texts and the "Points" you want to pursue.

Review your Source Notes one at a time and follow these clues you have left for yourself. Some will go nowhere. They'll turn out to be inappropriate for the assignment or there won't be enough material to support an argument. Or, if you're pursuing a topic of your own interest, the ideas just don't seem as fascinating to you on the second encounter. But some thoughts you recorded will remain interesting, appropriate, and supportable. Bring them to a discussion. Write about them. What your instructor wants (if it's a course), what your readers will appreciate (if you're writing, what you'll thank yourself for in the future (if you're pursing your own questions) is evidence of your thoughtful response to the text and elaboration of that response into your own ideas.

A good discussion, essay topic, blog post, podcast, article, or book most often comes out of your response to an external stimulus such as a text. An interesting response deals with a basic question that isn't too easily answered but that isn't *so* large that it can't possibly be answered. This requires focus. A good topic, formulated in a few words, could become the title of your response and engage your audience immediately. If it's not meaningful to you, it's highly unlikely that you'll make it meaningful to your reader.

By now you should be beginning to see how these tasks – making notes, preparing for discussions, formulating a topic – all build on one another. The two authors who have contributed to this handbook have been, basically, lifelong students ourselves. We know from experience there is rarely time to go back and redo things. But if you put some effort into these steps as you go through them, your notes will generate ideas for discussion, either with other people or with yourself inside the note system (Luhmann referred to his *zettelkasten* as his "discussion partner"). Discussions will help you focus on the most promising interpretations, and you'll be on your way to a solid response. The worst thing for a student, professional, or motivated amateur is to be facing a deadline with no idea what you are going to say. If you work at each of these steps, that won't be a problem. The topic and probably a lot of the points you want to make, will jump out of your notes at you.

Discussion, either with others or yourself, is an ideal way to try out ideas and interpretations that will become Point Notes and might lead to output. When you write notes for discussion, they're for you. The ideas on your Source Notes can be half formed: questions you don't yet have answers to. Bouncing these ideas off a group (or yourself after a little time away from them) will help you develop them and will tell you which ones are most interesting to others and to yourself.

**Settling on a Manageable Topic**

At some point you may be asked to turn in a tentative essay topic, or you may set yourself a goal of making a plan to produce output. In a less open situation you may only be able to pick a topic from a set the instructor provides. In any case you should keep in mind that:

- Your purpose is to explore some specific part of an idea or a text and its relationship to some general idea you've interpreted;
- Your time (and your audience's time) is limited,

MAKE NOTES AND WRITE 63

so choose a topic that allows you to produce the output on time;
- Your composition requirement is typically set rather than open ended, if you are writing in a particular format such as an essay, article, blog post, or video script;
- Your readers have read usually read (or can read) the texts you've read, or are familiar with the material; they want your insights, not a summary.

Remember the scope: when you receive an assignment or take on a project, you are usually going to write a short interpretation of a specific topic. Not to resolve for all time how James Joyce's *Ulysses* changed the nature of the hero in modern novels or to trace all the influences of the French Revolution on the development of American nationalism. The scope of your project is most often pretty specific and it will naturally narrow some more, as you focus on what interests you. That's a good thing.

### An Example (from literature)

Imagine that when you were reading *The Odyssey* in a World Literature class, you found yourself interested in Homer's portrayal of women. You marked some passages, wrote comments in the margins of your text, paraphrased your thoughts into Source Notes, and brought them up in class. After clearing up the "facts" – who did what? when? how? and why? – maybe you still want to know: Why did I respond the way I did? What was Homer doing?

"Is there enough material to build an interpretation?" you ask yourself. More specifically: Who are the female characters Kirke, Kalypso, Nausikaa, Penelope, Helen,

Klytaimnestra, Eurykleia, Arete? Do they have anything in common? Differences? How does Odysseus seem to view them? Is his reaction consistent or does it vary? How do they respond to him? How does this affect Odysseus? How does their interaction relate to the world depicted in the text? How do they function in relation to the larger theme? Does any pattern emerge?

Once you've read, thought about, and discussed something that interests you, you are ready to pursue a general and still unshaped topic that is appropriate and certainly has enough material to investigate more closely and develop a description of "Homer's Portrayal of Women in *The Odyssey*." This is probably not yet a manageable topic for a short paper, but it's already better than a more general topic like "*The Odyssey*." As you focus you might narrow your topic into a comparison of faithful wives to unfaithful wives, or of wives to mistresses, or of those women who provide security and continuity to those who offer adventure and experience. You might find that these categories are unsatisfactory to you. Good! Develop your own perceptions of how these characters function in the text.

### Another Example (from social science)

Now imagine that in a US History class you are given an assignment: Compare Booker T. Washington's approach to race relations in his 1895 "Atlanta Exposition Speech" with W. E. B. Du Bois's approach in *The Souls of Black Folk* (1903). You read the two texts and discover that Du Bois is highly critical of Washington, and *Souls* is his counterargument to Washington's position.

But as you read Du Bois's criticism of Washington and go back to the "Atlanta Exposition Speech" to see if that's really what Washington said, you find yourself feeling one way or another about the debate. Maybe you think Du Bois misrepresented Washington's position. Maybe you think Washington was a realist and Du Bois was an idealist. Maybe you agree with Du Bois that Washington was an appeaser. Maybe (best case) you become aware as you read and discuss the ideas with others or in your notes that different people have reacted in all these ways to the texts. Now you've got the basis of an essay that can look at both texts, discuss the variety of reactions to them, and then – if you choose to – stake out a claim of your own. Even though your topic was assigned to you, with a little thought you can take it in a direction that interests you and that will allow you to build your own interpretation.

The important point in both examples is that once you've read a text carefully and made good notes, you can begin the process of making the ideas your own and making an original contribution by bringing your experience and imagination to bear on a central idea – a topic – that especially interested you. Your notes will lead you back to the areas that caught your attention as you wrote them. Most of the time you'll find your topic there. You can test out and refine that topic in discussion, and see how others respond to it. As you work with it, you may find that there's something in particular you want to say about this topic. That particular something will be the thesis of your response, which we'll discuss later.

Making Point Notes

The basic building blocks of your own output are ones where you have not only summarized and paraphrased the information you received from another source, but you've analyzed it, interpreted it, and have something to say about the idea it contains. Others have called these "Main Notes" or "Permanent Notes" or "Evergreen Notes". I called them Point Notes to remind myself that when I write them I should be *making a point*.

In many fields there are data points or pieces of evidence, and then conclusions that you draw or support by using them. When I save them in my notes, the pieces of evidence are usually Source Notes and the argument they support is described in a Point Note. Sometimes this Point is as direct as something like "If X is true (cite card for X) and Y is true (cite card for Y), then Z must be true." Or "The argument presented by A is contradicted by those of B and C. Here's a way of understanding that disagreement."

> Connections / hot nodes  3.1.2.3/3
>
> One of the features touted about the Zettelkasten is that you "find" connections and your interests in it, rather than forcing them. However, this is work at the beginning. esp. making the connections.

Often a Point Note describes a connection between two thoughts and creates a new idea bridging those thoughts. For example, when I was preparing for this section I wrote a Source Note that said "Luhmann read with his slip-box in mind". Luhmann said this himself and many scholars studying his system have mentioned it.

On another I noted that connecting one note to another and "being able to back-trace an idea to its source is critical". As I was reviewing these I wrote the Point Note pictured, continuing the train of thought that advocates of the *zettelkasten* system often claim it "shows" you what some people call "hot nodes", which can tell you (sometimes surprising) things about the topic you are pursuing. This would be a very positive outcome, which helps explain why so many enthusiasts are trying to perfect a system that will help produce these insights.

I think claims of magical moments of "emergent complexity" where the note system reaches some sort of critical mass and begins spitting out answers like an oracle are probably exaggerated. They sound a bit too much like the Singularity. But it's also true, I suspect, that by reviewing our notes regularly, comparing Source Notes and making Point Notes out of them, and diligently connecting new ideas into the train of thought they emerged from, we'll create a tree that will have more branches and leaves in some places than in others. Those branches will be where the action is; where we can expect to find a lot of material we can turn into output.

Writing a Point Note about an idea can trigger a cascade of other thoughts that you can explore on their own (and write additional notes about). These are the types of discoveries you might miss if you don't make the effort to write the first note and connect it to the system of thoughts. It's also true that creating a structure of folders (a process preferred by many digital apps) and dumping Source Notes into them without doing the additional work of interpretation probably fails to result in new insights. Apps that create a predetermined hierarchy of folders may also make it more difficult to follow your interests. The ability of these apps to "transclude" data or employ bi-directional links doesn't seem to answer this need — at least not without a steep learning curve! Doing the work of linking ideas together, whether in a digital or analog system, seems to be the only sure key to creating connections that will allow you to return in the future and follow the same trail of ideas.

# 7

# ORGANIZING OUTPUT

*My task...is, by the power of the written word, to make you hear, to make you feel – it is, before all, to make you see.* Joseph Conrad (1857-1924)

*Plans are worthless, but planning is everything.* Dwight D. Eisenhower (1890-1969)

After you have absorbed sources, written Source Notes paraphrasing and commenting on them, and turned these into Point Notes interpreting and analyzing the ideas you've chosen to pursue, what's next? Many note-taking apps and PKM systems are strangely silent on this question, since producing output isn't strictly within the scope of a knowledge management system. I was dissatisfied with this, because I'm not a collector of knowledge. I'm a teacher and writer. Also, this handbook began its life as a guide to writing; so it makes sense to continue to our goal.

At some point in your life, you've probably been told by a writing teacher that if the topic is the main idea, then the thesis is the main idea statement. You develop your topic, which begins as a word or a phrase (your subject), into a sentence (your subject plus a predicate, or what you have to say about it). But that's not enough, if you want the satisfaction of creating a fine thing or if you want to present your reader with an essay worth reading.

You're well past the "But I have nothing to say" stage. You have already begun the writing process by highlighting and making Source Notes, and you've reviewed those notes to discover your interests. You've explored possible topics in discussion and by writing Point Notes, and have settled on a manageable topic. Your close readings of passages relevant to your topic have suggested interpretations that need to be developed. It's important at the outset to dismiss any candidate for a possible thesis that is either factual or self-evident. Nothing obvious needs arguing, so a thesis that argues the obvious has no purpose. You don't want your audience to respond, "So what?" to output you've just gone to a lot of trouble to produce. You can prevent this by anticipating your reader's responses and asking yourself questions such as:

- What interpretation am I trying to persuade my reader is valid?
- What are my reasons for this interpretation?
- How is my interpretation different from other, accepted interpretations?
- What parts of the source material am I going to examine? To emphasize?

- What are my assumptions?
- Who would disagree? What objections can I expect? (If none, then do I have a thesis worth developing at all?)

A focused thesis statement connects a more general main idea with your specific development of it – in which you'll use concrete illustrations, observations, quotations, analysis, and interpretation. Thus, the topic sentences of your supporting paragraphs will be contained, explicitly or implicitly, in the all-important thesis sentence(s).

If you have read texts before beginning the note-making process described in this handbook, and then decided to adopt this process when you begin a formal "research" project, it might be necessary to return to some of your sources. In this case, rereading your texts with your topic in mind and organizing your evidence into Source and Point Notes helps you move from your initial, open-ended exploration of a topic to creating a thesis and ultimately supporting arguments. In other systems this stage is often called "brainstorming" or "freewriting" or "prewriting." It is imagined as an informal, personal part of the writing process. In the system I've outlined here, the process is still personal, but it's quite a bit more formal. The work you do in your Note-making system before you begin to write will prevent you having to grope for ideas and evidence when you're outlining and writing. And like producing the final output, this is also writing. You improve at anything by practicing it – this is another chance to practice writing.

An Example (from history)

Let's suppose one of your sources is James Loewen's

book, *Lies My Teacher Told Me*, for a course that deals with our changing ideas about history over time. In Chapter 6, which is titled "John Brown and Abraham Lincoln: the invisibility of antiracism in American history textbooks," Loewen says that history has mostly portrayed violent white abolitionist John Brown as insane, "narrowly ignorant," and "a religious fanatic." In contrast, Loewen says, "Consider Nat Turner, who in 1831 led the most important slave revolt since the United States became a nation. John Brown and Nat Turner both killed whites in cold blood…but unlike Brown, Turner is portrayed as…something of a hero."

You begin wondering, does Loewen make a valid point? What is the difference between John Brown and Nat Turner? Loewen cites his sources in the book, so you can look at them to see how the ways the two men are portrayed differs and how these portrayals have changed over time. Your topic, "Why is Nat Turner a Hero and John Brown a Villain?" will probably be controversial, but after bringing your questions to discussion and finding that your peers and instructor are interested in the direction you're taking this, you begin looking at other texts that mention Brown or Turner. Close reading reveals that many histories portray John Brown as ignorant, even though the record shows he was a highly educated man who had traveled in sophisticated social circles before Harpers Ferry. You review your Source Notes, write Point Notes about them, and begin to form an interpretation: maybe history can forgive Nat Turner for his killings because he was an escaped slave acting in a manner expected of his peer group, while John Brown was considered a traitor to his white, educated peer group. There are other possible interpretations, but you

MAKE NOTES AND WRITE    73

decide to test the thesis that "John Brown is vilified by history because Brown's certainty that Christianity and slavery were incompatible was an intolerable challenge to the smug rationalizations of other whites in 19th century America."

This will be a controversial thesis to explore – you've already run into many histories that implicitly or explicitly deny this interpretation. The upside is that you'll have the full attention of your audience. As you continue your research, you may find there were other factors leading to history's rejection of Brown, or that not all histories rejected him. You'll have an opportunity to refine your thesis – it's not carved in stone – but for now it's a good source of direction for your project.

### Another Example (from literature)

Returning to the previous imaginary World Literature class, suppose you decide to pursue "Homer's Portrayal of Women in *The Odyssey*". Class discussion reflected on the emphasis on "family values" in recent news coverage of politicians looking for issues near election time. Perhaps you were stimulated by what the pundits had to say. Or maybe you were offended by the superficiality of the "soundbites" – after all, you had just read Odysseus telling Agamemnon in Book Eleven that "empty words are evil." So you decide to take a closer look at families in the text. You reread relevant passages, making notes paraphrasing (Source Notes) and analyzing (Point Notes) the relationships of Odysseus-Penelope-Telemakhos on one side, and Agamemnon-Klytaimnestra-Orestes on the other.

You plan to contrast the "functional" families in *The Odyssey* with the "dysfunctional" ones, focusing on the role the wives play. You know you won't use those terms in your final draft, as they're both jargon and clichés, but they will get you started. It would be too obvious merely to point out that Penelope and Klytaimnestra represent "good guys" versus "bad guys." That's a "So what?" paper. As you analyze your Source Notes, you notice that Penelope is not such a one-dimensional character; neither is Klytaimnestra. You sense that Odysseus's wife's "fidelity" is motivated by causes more complicated than conventional, and Agamemnon's wife's "infidelity" is grounded in his sacrifice of her daughter for his brother's honor. Now you're interpreting and you know someone will disagree, so you prepare an argument. Your (tentative) thesis statement is: "Although some have proposed that *The Odyssey* was presented as an educational model prescribing rules and roles for generations of Greeks, a closer look at the characters of Penelope and Klytaimnestra suggests that Homer was as much a probing psychologist as a patronizing pedagogue." Okay, the alliteration might be a bit much – but you'll worry about that in a later draft; this is a good start. This thesis is also a bit too general: ultimately you'll have to be more specific as to which psychological aspects of these characters Homer probes. But it will serve to focus your thinking and help you develop your argument.

You can (and often do) change both your attitude and your plan as you explore sources and your responses to them. As that happens, you refine or revise your thesis. Your original statement is meant to function as your guide; it directs your writing, but it serves *your* purposes.

The two forms of logical arguments you'll probably end up using, depending on the source material and your goal for the output, will be deductive and inductive. A deductive argument might begin with evidence from sources or from previous interpretations, and lead to a specific conclusion in a format like this: "if A is true, and B is true, then C ought to be true." In the real world, A and B are almost never absolutes that no one is going to challenge, so your conclusion is always going to be tentative. The other option, an inductive argument, would begin with specific data and try to generalize from them, to a conclusion about the broader world. Its conclusion would also be tentative, but that's no reason not to argue your point strongly and with conviction.

As you read and research, your goal is to find the building blocks of your argument: factual data, prior interpretations you can comment on, and your own experience. As you analyze your Source Notes and write Point Notes, you'll want to organize your argument into a series of points that develop your thesis and that build upon each other to support your conclusion. Ernest Hemingway once said that good prose is architecture, not interior decorating. He meant that it is constructed on a solid foundation – it's graceful, but not primarily designed to be pretty. Since we're using an architectural metaphor, we might also want to remember architect Louis Sullivan's advice, that "form follows function." The mechanical structure that supports your ideas does not necessarily have to be apparent to the reader (viewer, listener, audience). But it has to be there. Its purpose is to help shape your argument so the reader can understand and follow it. Without a structure, your reader would quickly become lost, wandering through a random pile of "Oh, by the way" points that lead nowhere.

It might help at this point to begin an outline. An

outline is an opportunity to take all those individual building blocks of information you have been accumulating and start assembling them into a structure. Your main points will become the topic sentences that will control your middle paragraphs. They can be organized chronologically, in series of cause-effect pairs, or in any way your topic suggests. The logic of this organization will be contained in, or at least implied by, your thesis statement. They're also typically the topics of the Point Notes you choose to use to build this output. They give coherence to your argument by connecting with each other as well as with the thesis sentence in your first paragraph and with the concluding sentence in your last paragraph. So you could start by writing these controlling ideas down in a preliminary outline. If you have made good notes, often outlining is as simple as arranging your note cards in a logical order, and then transcribing the content of the notes. Or, if your notes are digital, cutting and pasting.

I like to imagine all the thoughts and ideas I've collected in my system of notes as a forest. I imagine it as three-dimensional, because the trains of thought I've been working on for some time look like trees, with branches of argument, point, and counterpoint and leaves of source-based evidence. Actually, the forest is four-dimensional, because it changes over time, growing as I add more to it. A piece of output I make using this forest of thoughts is like a path through the woods. It's a one-dimensional narrative or interpretation that starts at one point, moves in a line or an arc (sometimes a zig-zag) through the woods, touching some but not all of the trees and leaves. I like this imagery, because it suggests there are many ways to move through the forest.

The path I have chosen is one of these. Tomorrow I may choose another way to get to the same place, or decide to go to a different destination. I may touch some of the same trees on the way to that different destination (another reason to number notes so they can be located in different contexts!), or a new and different set of ideas and evidence. Either way, the whole forest is available to me for anything I may want to do.

If the arguments in your Point Notes are strong and complete enough, and you have enough evidence in your Source Notes, you may feel you just want to get on with the writing. Another possibility might be to write your rough draft first, and then try to outline it to verify that it makes sense. Either way an outline, no matter how sketchy, helps to ensure that your essay is going somewhere and not just bouncing around or spinning in circles. You are likely still going to reread, reconsider, add, subtract, rearrange, revise. At this point everything is tentative. A logical outline could be just the control you need to turn a rough draft into output that's a model of clarity. In expository, analytical media, your audience is not looking for baroque flourishes (we return to the architecture metaphor once again!). Whether you develop your argument by defining, describing, exemplifying, classifying, comparing, or contrasting, your audience is looking for insights. You have a reader, listener, or viewer for whom you must define your terms, expose your premises, and state your purposes. Doing this clarifies the scope and course of your argument for both of you.

Even when you make a logical argument that appeals to your audience's reason rather than to their emotions, your output's success is not simply a question of your argument being either "right" or "wrong." Your work will be more valid and persuasive if you have developed it cogently and communicated it effectively. Just as you look for author biases in texts, your audience naturally assumes that your interpretations are probably not completely impartial or absolutely objective. However, your arguments can and should be interesting and plausible. That's what "good prose" is. But this is the goal of your final draft, so don't expect it to happen all at once. Work toward it.

Settling on a useful structure, you'll want to keep in mind that your purposes are first, to set up a writer-reader (speaker-listener, presenter-viewer, etc.) relationship; second, to make your argument understandable, interesting, persuasive, compelling. Your organization will emphasize the material you think is important by controlling the sequence in which information is revealed. The shape you give your "building" depends ultimately on your goals and priorities, as the builder. But don't forget that architects design structures for other people. Your audience has to find a home in them as well. The basic structural model that works pretty well in many cases looks like this:

- General Introduction: get your reader's interest right away; briefly provide only necessary background (Don't summarize!). Make your topic clear; focus on a specific statement of your thesis.
- Organize supporting ideas into coherent paragraphs with clear topic sentences (this applies both to written works and to the scripts of audio and video productions).
- Create meaningful and smooth transitions

between paragraphs. Try to vary your sentences so they are not monotonous.
- Support every assertion you make with evidence from a credible source or a comparison of several.
- Connect all the ideas in your conclusion. You might want to move from a specific statement of the point you believe you have proven back to a more general discussion, reversing the order of your first paragraph, while adding a "so what" statement. This creates symmetry.

Abandoning the architecture metaphor for a moment, you could also think of this structure as a journey. You and your audience meet in the introduction. You go out together and have an adventure in the body paragraphs. Then you come back home and reflect on what it meant in the conclusion.

Of course, this is not the only way to structure your output. Different goals lead to different journeys; to different buildings, if we return to the architecture metaphor. If you're building a different building and it's working – that is, if your audience finds your output interesting and effective – then by all means stick to it and build on it, improving it all the time. Your readers, listeners, or viewers will give you the most meaningful feedback. Whatever you're producing, it will ultimately need to communicate your thoughts to your audience. Organization helps, so in a class or workshop your instructor or peers will be looking for (judging, grading) criteria such as: logical sequence; whether the theme keeps moving; good paragraph structure; smooth transitions; main ideas given proper emphasis; all generalizations supported; all paragraphs come out of the thesis and lead to the conclusion. Ultimately, one of the best compliments that can be given to good prose is that it did not get in the way of a cogent argument or a compelling narrative.

# 8

# COHERENT PARAGRAPHS

> *Get it down. Take chances. It may be bad, but it's the only way you can do anything really good.* William Faulkner (1897-1962)

> *You wouldn't hand in a lot of sticks and boards bunched together and call it a table. It's no better to hand in a detached bundle of statements starting nowhere in particular, training along and then fading out – and call it a theme.* Dorothy Canfield Fisher (1879-1958)

In the next few chapters, we're going to focus quite a bit more on the *writing* process. Whatever the final form of your output, unless it's visual art or improv, it will usually involve a written essay of some kind. Even an "extemporaneous" speech or lecture will benefit from preparation. Our assumption is that you have studied enough sources and made enough Source and Point Notes that you have sufficient material to produce an effective argument or narrative. The task now is to make that article or story as clear, easy to understand, and compelling as possible.

When you think about it, there's no contradiction in the advice of the two American writers quoted above. You should respond with genuine feeling and without inhibition to sources and ideas that stimulate you. But feeling isn't enough. When Gustave Flaubert asked, "Has a drinking song ever been written by a drunken man?" he meant a *coherent* song. Between "getting it down" and "handing it in", good writers show respect for their readers by organizing their material into recognizable patterns. One obvious way to do this is to work on "drafts"; sometimes it is useful to let a little time pass between completing a draft and revising it. An important benefit of taking your time is that by distancing yourself from your ideas you may be able to react to them more like your audience. In the heat of the moment when you are writing, you know what you meant by a particular phrase or argument. After some time has passed, you can see better, what you actually said. This helps insure you have shaped what might have begun as nebulous feelings into clear thoughts.

This brings us to the well-known (but perhaps not well *enough* known) basic unit of composition, the paragraph. It might not be exaggeration to say the paragraph is really the basic unit of thought. It contains a point or a claim, supported by argument, evidence, elaboration, examples. The traditional and still useful rule that a paragraph must have *unity, coherence,* and *emphasis* only means that it must make sense, that the sentences should fit together smoothly, and that not all the sentences function in the same way.

When you appreciate that its purpose is to support your thesis by *developing* and *connecting* your ideas meaningfully, then paragraph structure should appeal to your common sense. As a point of emphasis, the *topic sentence* – whether you choose to put it at the beginning, middle, or end – allows you to control your writing and guide your audience by expressing the main idea of the paragraph. Unless you are writing a mystery novel, there will be relatively few instances in your output when you'll want to *surprise* your reader.

Must every paragraph have a topic sentence? Not necessarily: if the main idea is obvious, then a topic sentence may be omitted. But even if it is only implied by your paragraph, you and your reader should have no trouble stating the main idea. Whether explicit or implicit, the topic sentence of each of your paragraphs should come out of your thesis statement and lead to your conclusion. Like the paragraph, the whole essay should have unity, coherence, and emphasis. *Try this:* next time you read an essay, underline only the topic sentences of each paragraph; then reread only what you've underlined. In many cases you'll see that the underlined sentences make up a coherent paragraph all by themselves (this is an easy way to write an abstract, incidentally). That's because most topic sentences are more specific than the thesis statement that generates them, but still more general than the supporting sentences in the paragraphs that illustrate them. They are the main points in the argument or story promised in the thesis statement; transitions between the writer's promise to the audience and the keeping of that promise.

No matter how important your message might be, it must also be understandable. Structure it for your reader!

## Examples: Opening Paragraphs

From a student essay discussing Kafka's *The Metamorphosis*:

> When Nietzsche declared that "God is dead," he did so with an air of optimism. No longer could man be led about on the tight leash of religion; a man liberated could strive for the status of Overman. But what happens if a man refuses to let go of his "dead" God and remains too fearful to evolve into an Overman? Rejecting the concept of the Christian God means renouncing the scapegoat for the sins of man and accepting responsibility for one's own actions. In *The Metamorphosis* Gregor Samsa plays the god-like role of financial provider for his family. However, when his transformation renders him useless in this role, the rest of Samsa's family undergoes a change of its own: Kafka uses the metamorphoses of both Gregor and his family to illustrate a modern crisis.

*Some comments on the structure:* This introduction begins with two provocative introductory sentences, then a transition question and a response that presents the central idea of the essay. Next, the writer identifies the text and characters under discussion. Finally, the topic sentence of the paragraph, which, as the thesis statement, promises an interpretation. A paragraph such as this engages the reader's interest right away and makes the reader *look forward* to the rest of the essay.

From a student essay on the question, "What Do Historians of Childhood Do?"

> In his 1982 book *The Disappearance of Childhood*, Neil Postman argues that the concept of childhood is a recent invention of literate society, enabled by the invention of moveable-type printing. Postman says as a result of television, literate adulthood and preliterate childhood are both vanishing. While Postman's indictment of TV-culture is provocative, he ignores race, class, ideology, and economic circumstance as factors in the experience of both children and adults. Worse, he ignores history, making sweeping generalizations such as the claim that the pre-modern Greeks had no concept of children. These claims are contradicted by the appearance of children in classical Greek literature and in the Christian Gospels, written in Greek, which admonish their readers to "be as children." A more useful and much more interesting observation might be that the idea of childhood and the experience of young people has changed significantly since ancient times, and continues to change.

*Some comments on the structure:* Like the previous example, this essay begins with a statement from a text (this time with a paraphrase rather than a quotation) and builds towards a thesis statement. In this case the build-up, where the student writer disagrees with one of the texts used in the class, is stronger than the thesis. The writer has not stated exactly what he will argue, aside from suggesting he finds at least some of the ideas of childhood advanced in the course materials unsatisfactory. Keeping the reader in suspense may add to the interest of the essay, but in a short paper it might also waste valuable time and leave the reader unsure whether the writer has really thought things through.

From an essay on *Crime and Punishment*:

> "Freedom depends upon the real...It is as impossible to exercise freedom in an unreal world as it is to jump while you are falling" (Colin Wilson, The Outsider, p. 39). Even without God, modern man is still tempted to create unreal worlds. In Feodor Dostoevsky's *Crime and Punishment* Raskolnikov conceives the fantastic theory of the "overman." After committing murder in an attempt to satisfy his theory, Raskolnikov falls into a delirious, death-like state; then, Lazarus-like, he is raised from the "dead." His "resurrection" is not, as some critics suggest, a consequence of his love for Sonya and Sonya's God. Rather, his salvation results from the freedom he gains when he chooses to live without illusions.

*Comments:* Once more, a stimulating opening. Between the first and last sentences, which frame the paragraph (the last one, as well as being the thesis sentence, is the specific application of the generalization in the first sentence), the writer makes her transition to the central idea and introduces the text and character she wishes to discuss. The reader is given enough information to know what to expect. It promises to be an interesting essay.

Each of these writers above chose to open with a quotation or reference that helped focus the reader's attention and reveal the point of view from which a specific interpretation will be made. Movement from the general to the specific is very common in introductory thesis paragraphs, but it is not obligatory. You can begin with your thesis statement as the first sentence; start with a question; or use the entire opening paragraph to set the scene and provide background, then present your thesis in the second paragraph. The field is wide open to make choices and even create new options, so long as your sentences *move* to create a dominant impression on the reader.

Your first paragraph presents both your topic and your attitude, to an audience that is potentially sympathetic but doesn't know you yet (even if they are familiar with you as a person or from other output, they don't yet know the stance you are taking as author of *this* work). Create the impression right away that both the topic and you deserve serious attention. Your audience should feel like companions, not captives, on your journey of exploration. Take the lead; be clear; be interesting.

### Examples: Middle Paragraphs

From a student essay comparing P'u Sung-ling's (17th century) *The Cricket Boy* and Franz Kafka's (20th century) *The Metamorphosis*, two stories that deal with a son's relationship to his family. The writer's thesis was that according to these authors, one must connect in meaningful ways with other human beings in order to achieve what Virginia Woolf calls "health," "truth," and "happiness."

> The most obvious similarity between Kiti and Gregor is that they both take the forms of insects; however, their and their families' reactions to the changes account for the essential difference between the characters. Whereas Kiti thinks a cricket represents "all that [is] good and strong and beautiful in the world (*Cricket Boy*, p. 2), Gregor is repulsed by his insect body and "closes his eyes so as not to have

to see his squirming legs" (*Metamorphosis*, p, 3). Their situations also affect their families differently. Kiti's experience serves as a catalyst that brings his family closer together: "For the first time, his father had become human, and he loved his father then" (*CB*, p. 2). Gregor's transformation, on the other hand, succeeds in further alienating him from his family: his parents "could not bring themselves to come in to him" (*M*, p. 31). While Kiti and his parents develop a bond based on understanding and mutual respect, Gregor becomes not only emotionally estranged from his family, but also physically separated from them.

*Some comments on the structure:* This writer is clearly on her way, with specific examples from the texts, to supporting her argument concerning the need for self-respect and communication. Notice that she uses transitions such as "however," "whereas," "also," "on the other hand," while," and "not only..., but also..." to connect her thoughts and make her sentences cohere. Transitional words and phrases are the glue both within and between paragraphs: they help writers stick to the point, and also allow readers to stay on the path the writer intends.

## Transitions

***Only connect!*** E.M. Forster (1879-1970)

Writers use transitional words and expressions as markers to guide readers on their shared exploratory journey. Transitions can express relationships very *explicitly*, which is often exactly what is needed. However, experienced writers can also build more subtle bridges between ideas, hinting at relationships with *implicit transitions*. These relationships may change from vague initial impressions to a very concrete statement as the argument develops, allowing the reader to "discover" the writer's conclusion as the essay builds to its final paragraph.

Types of explicit transitional expressions

- **Comparison**: *such as, like, similarly, likewise, in the same way, in comparison, correspondingly, analogous to*
- **Contrast**: *but, however, in contrast, although, different from, opposing, another distinction, paradoxically*
- **Cause-effect**: *because, as a result, consequently, for this reason, produced, generated, yielded*
- **Sequence**: *initially, subsequently, at the onset, next, in turn, then, ultimately*
- **Emphasis**: *above all, of major interest, unequivocally, significantly, of great concern, notably*
- **Examples**: *for example, in this instance, specifically, such as, to illustrate, in particular*
- **Adding points**: *as well as, furthermore, also, moreover, in addition, again, besides*

Sometimes we find we are overusing explicit connectors and our transitions are beginning to feel mechanical. How many times have we used "furthermore" or "however"? How many "other hands" do we have? We can improve the flow of our writing either by changing up the transitional expressions, or by shifting toward more implicit transitions. One technique is, in the first sentence of the new paragraph, refer (either explicitly or implicitly) to material in the preceding paragraph. Some examples:

> When Alcibiades does give his speech, we see that his example is Socrates himself.
> While this interpretation still seems reasonable, I was surprised at the difficulty of uncovering useable data in the records of past societies.
> This sometimes sickening detail that Dante uses to draw the reader emotionally into the Inferno also stimulates the reader to think about what he or she feels.
> The Greek system is much more relaxed; obeisance and respect for the gods is not required, although in most cases it seems to make life easier.

Each of these implicit transition sentences builds on the previous paragraph and calls for support in the new paragraph. Even more subtle (that is, more difficult) would be to make the *last* sentence of the paragraph indicate the direction the next paragraph will take. If you try this, be careful you do not at the same time change the subject. *You do not want to introduce a new idea at the end of a paragraph and destroy its unity.* Since it suggests a change in direction, we see this device used most commonly with thesis sentences at the end of introductory paragraphs.

Other examples of the "hinges" writers use to make connections between ideas include pronouns referring back to nouns in the previous sentences or paragraphs and synonyms to avoid repetition and overuse of pronouns. A good rule is not to overuse any device. In general, your transitions should not draw attention to themselves and distract your reader; they should help your argument flow as smoothly and logically as possible.

## Concluding Paragraphs

From another student essay on *Crime and Punishment*:

> Raskolnikov finally finds a new life: Indeed he [is] not consciously reasoning at all; he [can] only *feel*. Life [has] taken the place of logic and something quite different must be worked out in his mind. (Epi. II, p. 464) Thus he ends his suffering by abandoning intelligence and reasoning. Jean-Jacques Rousseau said that "above all the logic of the head is the feeling of the heart." Ultimately, Raskolnikov transcends the "logic of the head" by discovering love and freedom.

*Some comments on the structure:* The paragraph works well as a conclusion because you can tell immediately that the writer has said all that she wants to say about the subject. She uses a quotation from another source, to "rub up against" Dostoevsky, expanding the dialogue between the text, the writer, and the reader by adding another voice. The answer to the "so what?" question is implied in the last sentence: love and freedom are values we all can share. Note that although this is a different conclusion from that of the earlier essay discussing *Crime and Punishment*, both interpretations are interesting and valid because both writers supported their arguments with careful readings of the text.

From a History essay analyzing the influence of Philippe Ariès's book *Centuries of Childhood* on later historians:

> In the end, *Centuries of Childhood* did not establish

a conceptual framework for children's history. Nor did the rival philosophies of history create a new paradigm for children's history. Ariès identified a subject of study. He was a prospector who uncovered a rich vein of material. Subsequent miners should use whatever tools and techniques are best suited to getting the ore out of the ground. Historians should stop fighting over theories and get to work uncovering the lives of children and families. This will involve, as Jordanova suggested, self-awareness and sensitivity. But it should not be sidetracked by ideological debates. As Cunningham observed, the stakes for modern children and families are high. To make children's history useful for the present, historians of children and families need to put aside their differences and get back to work.

*Some comments on the structure:* As in the previous example, the writer includes the perspectives of other commentators. This is especially common in essays on secondary sources in history, because "historiography" is often imagined as an ongoing conversation about primary and important secondary texts. The "so what" statement is more explicit this time, relating the study of children in the past to improving the lives of children and families today. The importance of connecting with the needs of today is problematic (many historians would criticize this as "presentism"); so the writer includes a supporting perspective from a sympathetic commentator.

From a Literature essay in which the writer compares and contrasts the character she is examining with a character from another work:

> Like Ophelia, Gretchen has moments of confusion and despair, but she decides to give in to her feelings

and take responsibility for them. By having Gretchen freely stay behind to face her execution, Goethe casts aside any similarities that his character shares with Shakespeare's Ophelia. Along with the empowering freedom of Gretchen's striving comes the struggle to act rightly. But if no objective absolutes exist, according to Goethe's God, on what basis can Gretchen make her decisions in order to be saved? She comes to the realization that the only absolutes exist within herself. Goethe's God saves her, not for being a penitent Christian, but for staying true to these self-imposed absolutes.

*Some comments on the structure:* Another strong conclusion. The writer's interpretation could be contested, but she has argued it well and convincingly throughout the essay and concluded strongly. Incidentally, note also that by specifying "Goethe's God" in her interpretation she avoids any distracting discussion of religion and keeps her writing focused on literary analysis. We don't argue the nature of "God" in an essay about literature; only the nature of the "God" in the text.

These basic units of composition we call paragraphs are used to introduce, support, and conclude your thesis. Remarkably, their structure and function remains pretty much the same, whether we are writing a five-paragraph essay or a 350-page dissertation. If we use them skillfully, our reader or audience should understand our position and be able to follow the progress of our ideas. If we are "going somewhere" with our argument or narrative, our transitions will appear natural and smooth. Our output can have any number of paragraphs, so long as they connect with our thesis and with one another. Finally, since they unfold in time (whether they are consumed as text, audio, or video) paragraphs allow us to deal with ideas sequentially. Don't try to juggle more than one point at a time. You'll confuse both yourself and your readers. These common-sense guidelines promote the much-prized "unity, coherence, and emphasis" your audience will sense in good paragraphs. Good paragraphs yield good essays.

# 9

# EFFECTIVE SENTENCES

*I see but one rule: to be clear.* Stendahl (1783-1842)

*The main thing I try to do is write as clearly as I can. Because I have the greatest respect for the reader, and if he's going to the trouble of reading what I've written – I'm a slow reader myself and I guess most people are – why, the least I can do is make it as easy as possible for him to find out what I'm trying to say, trying to get at. I rewrite a good deal to make it clear.* E. B. White (1899-1985)

In these two examples, a twentieth-century essayist/editor used three sentences to express what a nineteenth-century novelist/critic said in one. Which is the "better" piece of writing? The question is meaningless – or rather, it's badly formulated. The common-sense question to ask about writing is: How well does it *work*? To answer that, we should first consider two other questions: What does it intend to do? To whom is it addressed? (Recall that these were two of the questions we asked when evaluating sources at the beginning) A writer's purpose and audience quite naturally help to determine style, and we shouldn't be surprised to find Stendahl's writing often looking like the second example and White's writing like the first, when appropriate for their goals and audiences. Given the purposes and readers of each of these quotations, they both "work" equally well in their contexts.

If the rule for a paragraph is that it should have *unity, coherence and emphasis*, then the expectation for a sentence is that it should make sense. Let's look again at White's middle sentence. It expresses a half dozen ideas: his respect for the reader; his gratitude for the reader's "trouble"; his acknowledgement that he's a "slow reader" himself; his assumption that "most people are"; his obligation to clarify his thoughts; and his confession that he might not be able to fully express himself anyway. White could have written all that in six separate, precise sentences. But he chose to use a more personal, colloquial manner in order to engage his reader; to *show* his reader that writing, as well as reading, is a careful, thoughtful process. If you understood that (or if you *felt* that while reading his sentence), then White succeeded in writing a truly effective sentence. Indeed, his sentence obeys the "rule" to be clear just as well as Stendahl's short epigram. And as White suggests in his last sentence, that complicated middle bit was probably rewritten "a good deal" before it appeared in its final form. Notice too, how White brackets the long sentence with two short, concise ones to vary the pace of his unfolding argument and avoid overwhelming his reader.

In light of these two very different examples of sentences that both work, it might seem silly to try to identify the "ideal" sentence. There might be contexts you will write for that have different needs, but I think we can make some general assumptions about your audience and goals, that can then be modified as needed. We can say that *generally,* concrete nouns for your subject and active verbs introducing the predicate help your reader quickly grasp what you're talking about and what you wish to say about your topic. These work better than abstract nouns and passive verbs. *Generally,* it's more effective to modify your nouns and verbs with individual adjectives and adverbs rather than complicated phrases or clauses – simply because you don't want unnecessary words to weaken good ideas.

Consider this first paragraph from a student essay:

> What is a hero? Why do we admire certain people in our society? Since the beginning of time man has searched for someone to imitate and to use as a role model in his own life. In many ancient civilizations there is literature which centers on a hero of that time. But over time man has changed tremendously; or has he? No matter how advanced our civilization becomes, our heroes generally possess the same qualities and attributes. One of the oldest writings that modern man possesses, *The Epic of Gilgamesh,* is based on a hero and his adventures that he encounters during his lifetime. Although *The Epic of Gilgamesh* was written over 5,000 years ago, the hero Gilgamesh would still be a hero today. The reason why one may consider Gilgamesh a modern day hero

is because he is strong, sensitive, confident (yet humble), unselfish, and successful.

*Some Comments:* This paragraph is *not* particularly effective. Yet there is nothing structurally, grammatically "wrong" with the sentences. The ideas it contains are not extremely complicated. So why is it so difficult to read? Is it because irritatingly obvious unnecessary words and seemingly endless repetitions have weakened the ideas? Suppose we rewrite the paragraph without eliminating any of the *necessary* words and without changing any of the ideas the writer seems to have intended:

> People have always searched for role models, and the literature of many ancient civilizations center on a hero. Do our "heroes" today possess the same general qualities? Written over 5,000 years ago, *The Epic of Gilgamesh* recounts the adventures of a man who would still be considered a hero because he is strong, sensitive, confident (yet humble), unselfish, and successful.

Okay, we've reduced it from nine sentences, 147 words to three sentences, 61 words by pruning deadwood – but honestly, that still hasn't made us really excited to read the rest of the essay. To continue the "pruning" metaphor (and return to my "forest" metaphor): writing a good essay is like developing a framework of branches (topic sentences) that will act as a skeleton on which foliage, flowers, and fruit (your thoughts, arguments, conclusions) can grow. A better shape can produce more fruit and make that fruit easier to pick. But in the case above, will the effort be rewarded? Has the writer done enough of the groundwork to make this essay interesting and engaging?

In order to write well, you need to have something to say. Once you have something to say, you need to make the audience want to listen.

So how do sentences help us express worthwhile ideas in ways that will make people want to listen? Consider the main definition of "sentence" in *The American Heritage Dictionary*: A grammatical unit that is syntactically independent and has a subject that is expressed or…understood and a predicate that contains at least one finite verb. Being mechanically correct is certainly important – but it isn't enough. The kind of writing our audiences are expecting in our content should also have a point and a human *voice*. Maybe we should revive the obsolete definition of "sentence" mentioned in the same dictionary: An opinion, especially one given formally after deliberation. [Middle English, opinion, from Old French, from Latin…*sentire*, to feel].

In addition to conveying information and proving our familiarity with the sources, effective sentences should show our engagement with the material – how we *feel* about the issue at hand. This does not mean we don't have to offer a reasonable, logical argument. It means the audience needs to sense that we care about what we're saying.

Since the basic units of composition are paragraphs, the purposes of our sentences are to introduce, develop, support, explain, illustrate, and emphasize the main ideas as interestingly and economically – thus effectively – as possible. "Given formally after deliberation" doesn't have to mean impersonal and mechanical. In addition to giving ideas a human "voice", we should also express them with style.

For our purposes, style means no more than building

our sentences by choosing and arranging words so they clearly present our ideas about our subject. In the next chapter we'll discuss the appropriateness of words themselves; for now let's look at *sentence structure*. The interesting ideas, honest feelings, and thoughtful responses we have developed from our notes need to be revealed and developed in an *orderly* way so as to hold your audience's attention. Sentences that attract attention to *themselves* rather than to our ideas because of their awkwardness distract and cause the audience to lose confidence in our arguments.

## Active vs. Passive Voice

Using passive verbs (verbs of being) rather than active verbs (verbs of *doing*) is one of the most common mistakes made by writers at all levels. The sentence you just read is a passive sentence – no one does anything. *Sometimes* passive statements of fact are appropriate. But writers at all levels overuse "is," and we all need to write carefully and avoid this pitfall.

Why is active voice so important? What if we had ended the previous paragraph passively? We could have said, "The verb 'is' tends to be overused by writers. Passive voice is a problem that should be avoided by careful writers." If we had done this, the reader *might have* been left with the impression that what we're really interested is verbs. And that's not the case: what we're really interested in is *writing*.

Maybe history offers a clearer example. How often have you read passages in history textbooks like "The Declaration of Independence was written in 1776," or

"There were riots after the execution of the prisoners"? Do these sentences tell you the whole story? Did things *just happen*, or did somebody *do something*? In history, this is not just a question of style: it's a serious issue of interpretation. Overusing the passive voice, where things "just happen", denies people of *agency* and portrays a random world without cause and effect. It also insulates people from responsibility for their actions and short-circuits questions about motivation and differing points of view.

Yes, the passive voice often does sound more "authoritative" (or at least pedantic) because we've grown up reading textbooks written this way. Maybe "Hamlet was written between 1599 and 1602" doesn't sound that bad to you, but what if the passage instead read, "Shakespeare wrote Hamlet between 1599 and 1602"? Now we can visualize a man sitting down to do something, and we naturally begin to wonder, what was going on around him? Why did he write this play at that moment? What was he trying to say?

Similarly, rather than saying "there were riots" as if they just happened like rain from a cloudless sky, we might say "outraged by the execution of their friends and neighbors, farmers and city union-members rioted and attacked symbols of the state." This active construction opens the door to all kinds of possible questions about the situation and the parties involved. Of course, the active version requires the writer to *know more* information about the event than just the date when it "happened" (which may be why lazy textbook authors resist the active voice). And it also requires the writer to take a stand (which may be why some students avoid it).

Hopefully you can see that in addition to making our

writing much more interesting to read, using active verbs allows us to really explore our subjects. By writing actively, we can change a string of flat, dead facts into a series of actions and reactions. That means, a series of choices. That means a series of questions that may open new and interesting avenues for exploration.

## Common sentence problems

Confusing sentences distract the reader from the points we are trying to make. Here are examples of some of the most common mistakes, along with corrected sentences. You can catch most of these by reading your draft out loud and asking yourself (or a friend) if it makes sense.

The most common sentence problems are **FRAGMENTS** and **RUN-ONS**.

> "What am I going to do with my life?" A question everyone asks and can never answer.

*Connect the fragment*: "What am I going to do with my life is a question…

> Overall the English invasion was a complete success with some learning curves thrown in at the beginning, but for the most part, it was a complete and utter domination of the indigenous people.

*Separate the thoughts:* simplify the sentence and drop the qualifiers to divide these ideas and emphasize the "but." "The American colonies were a great success for the English, but they were an utter disaster for indigenous peoples."

> Knowing that death terminates all his problems in life, as well as all his joys, Hamlet recognizes that "the

> dread of something after death – the undiscovered country, from whose bourn no traveler returns."

*Still a fragment:* what's the object of "recognizes"? What's the predicate of "the dread of something after death"?

> They maintain a similar kind of distance verbally as well, the first words Odysseus and Penelope speak to each other are "strange woman" and "strange man," respectively.

*Separate the run-on.* Three possibilities:
1. *Two sentences:* ...verbally as well. The first words...
2. *Comma and conjunction:* ...verbally as well, and the first...
3. *Semi-colon:* ...verbally as well; the first words...

A related Subject-Predicate problem concerns **REPETITION** of the subject.

> It was not uncommon that different families would share certain abundant areas for everyone had equal right to the bounty. It was this idea of the native families that was probably what they were believing would be the case when deals were made with the English colonists.

*Trim, then combine these thoughts:* Native families commonly shared resources, and believed this sharing was protected in their contracts with colonists. (47 words to 16. And we got rid of the *passive voice*)

> For some of the pagans in Beowulf's culture, they believed in creating their own destiny.

*Don't complexify a simple sentence.* One subject, one

predicate. Some pagans in Beowulf's culture believed in creating their own destiny.

> Beowulf killed dragons. The fact that he killed dragons is what made him a hero. He achieved this status through the ability to overcome his fear.

*Eliminate repetition & contradiction:* Sentence 3 contradicts sentence 2. Maybe the writer meant: "Beowulf killed dragons, and became a hero by overcoming his fear." (26 words to 11)

Many sentence problems in essays are due to a lack of **PARALLEL STRUCTURE**.

> Dante finds himself lost in a dark wood and then Virgil led him out.

*Don't mix tenses:* either "finds—leads" or "found—led"

> They believed in having territories merely for the safety of their villages but the concept of owning the land itself for private gain didn't seem to be an ideology.

*Try not to change subjects:* "They" are the subject of first part, "the concept" is the subject of second (and there's that active-passive voice issue again). How about: "The natives held land to protect their villages, not for private gain."

> The Anglo-Saxons like to drink, hang around the mead hall, and fighting.

*Make parallel*: Either "liked to drink, hang around…and fight" or "liked drinking, hanging…and fighting."

MAKE NOTES AND WRITE   105

> Unlike the Christian philosophy of mourning a loved one, the pagans sought out revenge.

*Faulty comparison:* Christian philosophy should be compared to pagan *philosophy,* or Christians to pagans. Another way of thinking about it: Does my modifier clearly refer to what it is supposed to modify? "Unlike the Christian philosophy of mourning a loved one" *does not* modify "the pagans," but it *could* modify "pagan philosophy."

Without a clearly expressed **SUBJECT** and **PREDICATE**, your "sentence" merely confuses the reader.

> The static theme of Gilgamesh's quest for immortality is tested when the hero's only undefeatable conflict evolves into the sobering death of his beloved counterpart.

*Subject? Predicate?* Is the theme tested? What does "static" mean here? Is the quest tested? How? Does "undefeatable conflict" mean victory or defeat? This is very difficult to understand. Perhaps the reader means: "The death of his beloved Enkidu sobers Gilgamesh and stimulates his quest for immortality." Perhaps not. The *writer* should be interpreting this, not the reader.

> For Scott, gender must necessarily be a highly-dynamic concept, for her ultimate goal is the deconstruction of existing categories of analysis so that new (or hitherto unconsidered) historiographic themes—such as sexuality, family, identity, and, of course, gender—can be incorporated into the analytic methodology.

*Does the simple sentence buried here* (gender must

necessarily be a highly-dynamic concept) *mean anything?* The writer of this sentence was very unhappy he had to write a paper about Joan Scott's book *Gender and the Politics of History*. It shows.

> This scene give rise to many areas throughout the play.

*No specific predicate.* Areas could mean anything. Do platforms spring up all over the stage? Such a vague predicate can only irritate your reader.

These are just some of the ways you can make your sentences easier for your audience to understand and your argument more likely to be taken seriously. A really excellent, groundbreaking point or discovery can sometimes gain an appreciative audience despite being poorly expressed. But if we believe in what we have to say, why wouldn't we try to remove all the barriers we can to our message being widely heard and understood? Clear, compelling sentences remove barriers.

# 10

# APPROPRIATE WORDS

*The artist does not draw what he sees but what he must make others see.* Edgar Degas (1834-1917)

Hemingway: *I rewrote the ending to **Farewell to Arms**, the last page of it, 39 times before I was satisfied.* Interviewer: *Was there some technical problem there? What was it that had you stumped?* Hemingway: ***Getting the words right.***

**Words, words, words.** (Hamlet)

Making the reader see, "getting the words right," or as Hamlet put it in a different passage of the play, holding "the mirror up to nature," becomes increasingly difficult in a world facing accelerating change, clashing cultures, and serious questions about the nature of reality. Literature and History have led the humanities and social sciences in many of these challenges to old notions about language and meaning. But unless you're asked to write an essay about postmodernism or the "linguistic turn," your essays will probably not engage head-on with the cultural construction of language, identity, and reality. And even if you are interested in writing on these subjects, your output will still need to make sense to your audience.

The 1992 edition of *The American Heritage Dictionary* contained 16,000 new words that had not been in the first edition twenty-five years earlier. Its executive editor, Anne H. Soukhanov, said "the most important shift in English usage in 400 years [is] the pervasive change in words linked to gender." The advertisement for the fifth edition (in 2022 it has moved online, of course) boasts of an additional 10,000 new words. In addition to the gender-oriented changes, in recent years the dictionary has added "nerd", "passive smoking", "couch potato", "Mirandize", "job-sharing", "Burner", and "MacGuffin" as these new concepts demanded new vocabulary. Soukhanov recalled that 2,500 years ago Confucius had claimed it was impossible to know humans without understanding the power of words. We continue to re-create ourselves and our worlds with language.

Philosopher Ludwig Wittgenstein claimed, "The limits of my language mean the limits of my world." While it may not always be necessary for you to expand your world in order to complete an essay assignment, it *is* important to choose appropriate words. Remember that in addition to trying to earn some respect for your argument, you are always trying to hold onto and focus your audience's attention.

## Watch Out For

- *Unnecessary Repetition & Wordiness:* We often say more than we need to say. Voltaire is rumored to have apologized at the end of a long letter to his mother, saying "If I had had more time, I would have made it shorter." We'll come back to this when we talk about editing, but keep it in mind. Why say "at this point in time," when "now" will do? Remember the words of John Travolta's character in the movie *Get Shorty*: "I'm not going to say any more than I have to, if that."
- *Clichés* are overworked expressions such as "last but not least", "in my humble opinion", "lifestyle", "back to square one", and "in the final analysis." They give readers the impression that the writer is tired or doesn't care enough to keep the audience's interest with original thought. If the words are recycled, perhaps the ideas are as well.
- *Jargon* is technical or specialized language that quickly becomes clichéd, such as "wired", "out of the loop", the whole nine yards", "bottom line", "self-actualizing", "anal retentive", and "bourgeois." When jargon words are new and have specific technical meanings, they may not be understood by non-specialists; by the time they are well-known they have become clichés.
- *Pop culture references* tend to be more local and fleeting than elements of "high culture" that are recorded and taught as part of "cultural literacy."

Sometimes elements of popular culture become permanent (like the word "nerd" being added to the dictionary), but it's hard to tell just what will be preserved and when this will happen. "Poodle skirts", "Project Mayhem", "moon walking", "Hitchcock plots", "TANSTAAFL", and "Bears, Beets, Battlestar Galactica" might be obvious references and signals to a particular in-group – but usually we want our output to be understood by a wider audience.

- *Empty Words:* Vague generalizations such as "the people", "family values", "the American way of life", "liberal media bias", "the workers", "the humanist agenda", and "fake news" suggest that we haven't thought very hard about our subject, or that we're trying to sneak something by our audience.

Sometimes writers deliberately use words that lack specific meanings (*denotation*), not out of carelessness but for their ability to create subjective, non-rational responses in readers. Words have histories of their own, and many words are able to call on strong positive or negative associations. These *connotations* are often more important than the information the words provide. Habitual use of these words suggests either a high level of cluelessness (if the user isn't aware the subject is controversial) or a deliberate attempt to push the audience's emotional buttons and sabotage reasonable discussion. Examples include:

- *Words with Contested Meanings:* Like empty words, these are terms whose meaning has changed over time or words that have been

defined differently by competing groups. "Liberal", "conservative", "capitalist", "progressive", and "socialist" are obvious examples, but most general terms mean different things to different people. It's best to be as specific as possible: *Jefferson's* agrarian ideal, *Mary Lease's* populism, *Edward Bellamy's* utopian socialism, and *Hildegard von Bingen's* Christianity, for example.
- *Code-words:* Words that deliberately disguise what their users mean to say. Euphemisms hide the less acceptable elements of ideas (but from whom?); argot tries to create group identity and shared specialized knowledge. Some (controversial) examples include "Job-creators" (that is, the rich), "pro-life" (anti-abortion), "enhanced interrogation" (torture), "freedom fighters" (terrorists on our side), as well as more benign terms like "passed away" and "make love." Using code-words suggests that we share the point of view of others who regularly use them.

## Metaphors

Much (some people would say all) language is metaphorical. We use metaphors (implied comparisons) to connect the unfamiliar to the familiar, so that readers can "see, hear, feel" abstract concepts as if they were well-known everyday things. For example, most science texts fifty years ago still described atoms as little billiard balls, in spite of quantum mechanics which showed a hundred years ago that this metaphor was inaccurate. More recent science texts describe Einstein's gravity (curvature of space-time) as a metaphorical "rubber sheet" that massive objects create depressions in, so that planets spin around massive stars the way pennies circle the big funnel at the museum. This is a really complicated metaphor when you think about it – it tries to explain a nearly unimaginable process in four-dimensional space-time using a two-dimensional metaphor, the rubber sheet. A few things to keep in mind about metaphors when reading and writing:

- *Overextended metaphors:* The rubber sheet metaphor suggests one possible difficulty. Because most of us are not physicists, we are forced to rely on the assurances of experts that understanding this metaphor really tells us something about the way gravity really works in relativistic space-time. But even if it's a good, valid metaphor, it's still just a picture of a thing, not the thing itself. We need to be careful not to believe we "really know" the thing – or some vital detail that was not in the picture may jump out and metaphorically "bite us in the butt".
- *Misapplied Metaphors:* Because metaphors are often complex, we sometimes forget that they are "pictures" and try to use them where they don't belong. For example, the simple ideas scientists use to *describe* the complex theory of evolution are easy to misapply. When we say "survival of the fittest" and think we've understood the whole complex theory, then it's simple enough to take that idea and apply it to, say, people. The result of this particular error was called Social Darwinism, which was not

only bad science, but really bad for society.
- *Mixed Metaphors:* When we're using metaphors, it's important to stick with one at a time. Mixing metaphors can confuse the reader. The other examples were mostly for you to be aware of when reading – this one applies to your writing. Consider: "This chain of events burned Beowulf's bridges behind him." The alliteration is very Anglo-Saxon, but metaphorical chains can't burn metaphorical bridges. Or: "The Republicans, Democrats, and Independents in the Senate are just the flip side of a coin with nothing to choose from between them." But they can't be, because a coin only has *two* sides, and just one *flip side*. And the point was perfectly clear without the clunky coin metaphor. Even when physically possible, mixed metaphors usually paint an absurd picture. For example, "President Bush failed to subdue Iraqi insurgents. He could lead the horse to water, but when he couldn't make it drink the anti-war rats left his administration's sinking ship."

## A Few More Things to Watch Out For

- *Diction:* We can keep our audience motivated to follow our argument by choosing words with just the right shade of meaning and the right level of usage. Just as it's possible to be too dry and formal (which I'm trying to avoid in this handbook by adopting an informal, conversational tone – how's it working?), we should also try to avoid being too informal or vulgar. Although standards vary with different media, saying "Jefferson really screwed up the South with his hypocritical position on slavery" or "Hamlet wanted to get into Ophelia's pants" is probably not going to contribute to our argument or convince our reader we ought to be taken seriously – no matter how true each statement might be. Precise, appropriate writing suggests (and at the same time, encourages in our audience) precise thinking.

- *Sexist Language:* Remember that we are dealing with two "realities" in our writing: the perceived one outside ourselves and the one we are *creating* in our interpretation. The more personal our interpretation, the more important it is to gain our audience's sympathy so they will give us a fair hearing. Remember also that language not only *describes* a culture *as it is*, but also (intentionally or not) tends to *prescribe how it should be*. Sexist language is inappropriate and it is one of the quickest ways to needlessly lose the goodwill of a large segment of our audience. The problem arises from the lack of a common-gender third person pronoun in English. Americans are reluctant to use the English expression "one," as in: "One should improve one's mind." But it is no longer acceptable to use "man" to indicate humanity or "he" to indicate an unspecified subject.

One person's description is another person's prescription. Fifty years ago, a writer would have thought nothing of saying "one man's description." Does that change correlate with a change in the status of females in our culture? We can only hope so. So how do we write smoothly *and* gender-neutrally in spite of the missing pronoun? It's not that difficult – we've managed to get this far into the handbook without (hopefully) calling attention to the fact we haven't been using "he," "his," and "him" when not referring to an actual male person. Here are some techniques to try (use what feels natural):

- *Use the plural:* Instead of "A writer should choose his words carefully," try "writers should choose their words carefully." You can then continue with the gender-neutral plural, "they".
- *Use "you":* Instead of "If a person thinks about it, he will see…" try "If you think about it, you will see…"
- *Use "we":* similar to above: "If we think about it…" This can also subtly get us on the same "side" as the audience.
- *Try another form:* Instead of "When a person studies, he will improve his grades," try "Studying improves grades." You may notice that using these techniques also tends to make your writing more active and more personal.
- *Use a hybrid like "s/he":* This is much more acceptable than it was a few years ago, but will still trip up some readers, and you still have to decide what to do about object pronouns (her/him, hers/his). Many writers have chosen to use the feminine pronouns all the time. You probably don't have to be told that this could be seen as a political act, with results that may vary depending on the politics of your audience.

# 11

# REVISING

*How do I know what I think until I see what I say?*
E.M. Forster again

*I have never thought of myself as a good writer. Anyone who wants reassurance of that should read one of my first drafts. But I'm one of the world's great rewriters...It is, however, this hard work that produces a style.* James Michener (1907-1997)

This is the time to make sure that your well-reasoned, thoroughly supported, strongly-felt ideas become solid output. Just as wine must spend some time in the barrel, the bottle, and the glass before it's ready to drink, we must put our ideas into structured paragraphs, clear sentences, and appropriate words to prepare them for our audience and, if Forster is right, to be sure you really understand them yourself (Did you notice the metaphor and the parallelism there? Barrel to paragraph, bottle to sentences, glass to words).

## Examine the shape of your output:

- *Does it have a clear beginning, middle, and end?* Is our thesis introduced clearly, developed with concrete examples, and brought to a strong conclusion?
- *Have we anticipated our audience's questions and objections?* Have we addressed these concerns with convincing examples, data, analysis, and material from your sources?
- *Does all the evidence that we have presented belong in our argument?* Does each paragraph stick to the point and support our thesis? Do our points flow logically from our thesis to our conclusion? Are our transitions smooth?
- *Is our conclusion what we set out to prove?* Check it against the thesis statement. Have we stuck to our point?
- *Have we introduced a new idea along the way (especially at the end) that needs support?* If so, we might want to go back and make it part of our thesis statement. Or take it out and save it for another project.
- Beginning: Interesting introduction and clear thesis statement?
- Middle: Are we developing and sticking to our point with data or examples from our texts?
- End: Do we reasonably conclude our argument? Can the audience answer the question, "So what?"

## Specific Details

Just as proportion in our overall structure will help an audience follow our argument more easily, attention to the details of sentences and words will win their respect and help insure they will seriously consider our interpretation. Revising and editing our writing—*as many times as it takes*—is the hard work that produces a style. Handbooks and manuals like this one or Strunk and White's *The Elements of Style* can set us on the right path. But remember, Virgil could only get Dante through the Inferno; he couldn't get him into Paradise. At some point we'll have to leave our guide behind (after it has helped us avoid obvious errors) and make the positive creative choices that lead us to develop our own style.

But we're still here together, somewhere between the Inferno of the rough draft and the Purgatory of early revisions. So let's clear up those obvious errors. *Of course* we should use a spell-checker. It will flag or automatically correct the obviously misspelled words, but we still need to proofread for word choice. The spell-checker won't protect us from using the wrong word spelled correctly (using *except* when we meant *accept*, *effect* when we meant *affect*, *discreet* when we meant *discrete*, *site* when we meant *cite*, and even *pubic* when we meant *public*!). Proofread carefully. When in doubt, check the dictionary.

Here are some of the problems we find in many student essays over the years, and sometimes in our own early drafts, too:

### Lack of agreement between subject and verbs

*Faulty:* He reminds Dante that *each* of the sinners *have been* justly judged.

*Correct:* ...*each* of the sinners *has been*...

- *("Sinners" are not the subject, "each" is. Each is singular – as are everyone, anybody, someone, either, and neither.)*

*Faulty:* Hamlet's *search* for truth and understanding *reveal* his loss of faith.
*Correct:* Hamlet's *search...reveals*

- *Don't be confused by the phrase; the subject is singular.*

*Faulty:* The *limits* of language *makes* a profound impression on Descartes.
*Correct:* The *limits* of language *make...*

- *Plural subject needs a plural verb.*

### Lack of agreement between pronoun and antecedent

*Faulty:* A medieval *chronicle* usually included very violent events, but *they* rarely included graphic descriptions of violence.
*Correct: chronicles...they* or *chronicle...it*

- *"Chronicle" is the subject, not "events."*

*Faulty: Nobody* in Beowulf's band helped *their* leader fight the dragon.
*Correct: Nobody* in Beowulf's band helped *his* leader...

- *Although there were a lot of men in Beowulf's band, words such as "nobody", "anyone", or "somebody" are all singular.*

### Incorrect pronoun case

*Incorrect:* Socrates and *them* often met in the marketplace to debate.

*Correct:* Socrates and *they* often met...

- *We need a subject pronoun here. You wouldn't say "Them often met." But you could say "Socrates often met them in the marketplace..." if that was what you were really getting at.*

*Incorrect*: When Beowulf returned, the king gave *he* and his men rings and gold.

*Correct:* ...the king gave *him* and his men...

- *Object pronoun here. You wouldn't say "The King gave he rings and gold."*

### Subject and object pronouns

Singular: *He, she, and I* (subjects) wrote about *him, her, and me.* (objects)

Plural: *We and they* (subjects) painted a portrait of *us and them.* (objects)

### Use active verbs to correct:

*Boring facts:* King Charles was beheaded on January 30, 1649.

*Better:* Cromwell's victorious Parliamentary forces executed King Charles in a public beheading on January 30, 1649.

- *Now we can see that specific people deliberately did something serious to another real person, and we can begin to wonder who they all were and why they did* it.

**Tortured, unclear interpretation:** Raskolnikov's salvation is credited to his love for Sonya, but his will to love is the more fundamental emotion that saves him.
*Better:* Raskolnikov's *will* to love, more fundamental that his love for Sonya, saves him.

- *Now we don't have to wonder where that other opinion came from – we have the writer's strong statement to anchor us to this argument.*

**Confusing passive:** The witch is killed by Beowulf by having her head cut off.
*Better:* Beowulf decapitates the witch.

- *Now we know who did what to whom. The first was a weak description of such a violent act.*

**Wordy and weak:** Fire comes out of the dragon's mouth.
*Better:* The dragon breathes fire.

- *It did it deliberately, after all.*

**Something to Consider:** [The Carmel River] *rises* in the mountains, and *tumbles* down a while, *runs* through the shadows, *is dammed* to make a lake, *spills* over the dam, *crackles* among round boulders, *wanders* lazily under sycamores, *spills* into pools where trout live, *drops* in against banks where crayfish live. (John Steinbeck)

- *We are probably more concerned here, with writing output that is more like an essay than like fiction.*

*Still, we can learn something from this passage. Active verbs move writing along and carry the reader with them. Avoid "is..-ing" or is...-ed" constructions except where absolutely necessary. In this example it is appropriate that the river "is dammed" because the damming was not of its own volition. Active verbs, concrete nouns, straightforward word order, and minimal use of adjectives and adverbs constitute the* **style** *of this passage.*

### Mixed tenses

*Faulty:* In his new existence Gregor Samsa finds a modicum of freedom and enjoyed climbing on the walls. *Correct: finds...enjoys* or *found...enjoyed.*

- Choose a tense and then stick with it. This is obviously harder over a longer stretch of words than a single sentence and it's easy to switch tenses without noticing, especially if you are writing different parts of your essay at different times. When you are relating the details of a story told in a text, it is equally valid to use the present or the past tense. But you have to be consistent, so watch carefully!

### Misplaced or dangling modifiers

*Confusing:* Being more than half a god, we would expect to see a Gilgamesh who has knowledge, compassion, and wisdom that is above and beyond that of normal men.

*Clearer:* We expect to see in Gilgamesh, *who is two-thirds god, superior* knowledge, compassion, and wisdom.

- The clearer version puts the important point, "We

expect to see," at the beginning where the reader can't miss it, and it replaces the whole final phrase with the word "superior."

*Dangling:* Walking down to the second ledge, the voices of the damned arose.

*Clearer: Walking down to the second ledge,* Dante heard the voices of the damned.

*Or, if the voices are more important:* The voices of the damned rose *as Dante approached the second ledge.*

### Split infinitives

*Awkward:* Jeff asked Francesca to carefully explain her presence there.

Better: Jeff asked Francesca *to explain* her presence there *carefully*.

- *Interrupting an infinitive with a modifier distracts the reader.*

*Awkward:* As an escaped slave, Harriet Jacobs had to tearfully watch her children from a hidden crawlspace in a nearby house.

Better: Harriet Jacobs, an escaped slave, watched tearfully from a hidden crawlspace.

*Sometimes, although there may be someplace you could put the adverb that would "work" in the sentence, what's really called for is a more complete, concrete description of the emotion you're just brushing by with the adverb.*

### Faulty predication

*Incorrect:* The book says that...
*Even worse:* It says that...
*Correct:* The narrator says... or the author writes...

*Awkward:* Poetic justice is when the punishment fits the crime.

*Better:* Poetic justice *consists of the* punishment *fitting* the crime.

### Quotations

Alcibiades crowns Socrates as a man "whose words bring him victory over all men at all times" (*Symposium*, p. 98).

- *Use punctuation only if needed before the opening quotation marks. Closing quotation marks go after the exact quote and before the in-line reference (or footnote). Punctuation that doesn't end the sentence goes before the closing quotation mark. If there is no inline reference, end punctuation goes before the closing quote. If there is an inline reference, end punctuation goes after it.*

Socrates points out: "Men are quite willing to have their feet or hands amputated if they believe...those parts diseased" (p 85).

- *Use three dots ... (called ellipses) to indicate when you've left words out of the interior of a quote (not the beginning or end).*

Aeneas journeys to the underworld solely "to go to [his] dear father's side and see him" (*Aeneid*, VI, 162).

- *Use square brackets [ ] to show that you've added words. In this case, in the original quote Aeneas probably said "my".*

According to the text: In the original rough draft of the

Declaration of Independence, Jefferson wrote, "we hold these truths to be sacred and undeniable," but he changed to the familiar "we hold these truths to be self-evident" sometime before John Adams first saw the document.16

- *Block-quote (indent) passages that would amount to more than three lines of your paper. Do not use quotation marks around the block quote (which means you can use double quotes inside it if necessary). Put the inline citation or the footnote after the final punctuation.*

**Punctuation**

- Commas indicate a minor break in your train of thought, connect a subordinate clause to a main clause, or separate a series of items.
- *Use commas after introductory subordinate clauses.* When Dante descended into the pit, he feared for his life.
- Semicolons indicate a more distinct break in your thought; they separate independent clauses. Think of them as replacing a comma followed by "and".

*Faulty:* Gilgamesh had no equal, he became arrogant and cruel.

*More correct:* Gilgamesh had no equal; he became arrogant and cruel.

*Clearer:* Because Gilgamesh had no equal, he became...

- *Adding a subordinating conjunction makes one*

*clause dependent and helps the reader understand your point.*
- Periods show the end of a particular thought. That's why the British call them "full stops."

**Miscellaneous common errors**

- *Criterion* and *phenomenon* are singular; *criteria* and *phenomena* are their plurals.
- *Prophesy* is a verb. *Prophecy* is a noun. *Prophesize* is not a word!
- *It's* is a contraction for *it is*. *Its* (like *his* and *hers*) indicates possession and needs no apostrophe.
- Possession is shown by adding 's or s' to a word. The *book's* cover is singular; the *books'* covers are plural.
- Plural nouns get *'s*: *children's, people's*.
- Some writers add *'s* to singular nouns or names ending in *s*, others do not. Bill *Gates's* money is the same as Bill *Gates'* money.

# REVISION CHECKLIST

*Use this as a guide while revising and editing your essay. Check every item.*

1. \_\_\_\_\_Do I have an interesting introductory paragraph?
2. \_\_\_\_\_Is my thesis clearly stated? Is it arguable?
3. \_\_\_\_\_Does each of my middle paragraphs develop my thesis?
4. \_\_\_\_\_Do I support my argument with enough specific material?
5. \_\_\_\_\_Am I telling too much, and not showing enough?
6. \_\_\_\_\_Do I present more detail than is necessary?
7. \_\_\_\_\_Have I introduced extraneous material?
8. \_\_\_\_\_Am I retelling too much of the story?
9. \_\_\_\_\_Do I anticipate and address relevant counterarguments?
10. \_\_\_\_\_Does my conclusion follow from my thesis and argument?
11. \_\_\_\_\_Have I defended my position?
12. \_\_\_\_\_Did I oversimplify for the sake of closure?
13. \_\_\_\_\_Do I have logical transitions between sentences and paragraphs?

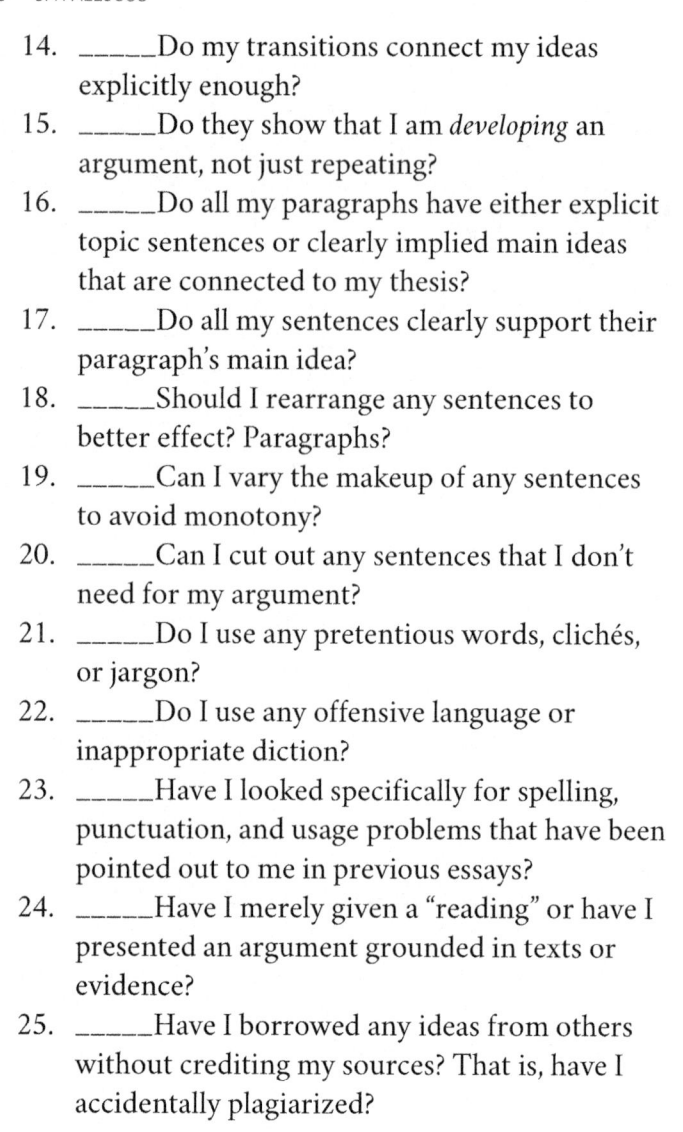

14. \_\_\_\_\_Do my transitions connect my ideas explicitly enough?
15. \_\_\_\_\_Do they show that I am *developing* an argument, not just repeating?
16. \_\_\_\_\_Do all my paragraphs have either explicit topic sentences or clearly implied main ideas that are connected to my thesis?
17. \_\_\_\_\_Do all my sentences clearly support their paragraph's main idea?
18. \_\_\_\_\_Should I rearrange any sentences to better effect? Paragraphs?
19. \_\_\_\_\_Can I vary the makeup of any sentences to avoid monotony?
20. \_\_\_\_\_Can I cut out any sentences that I don't need for my argument?
21. \_\_\_\_\_Do I use any pretentious words, clichés, or jargon?
22. \_\_\_\_\_Do I use any offensive language or inappropriate diction?
23. \_\_\_\_\_Have I looked specifically for spelling, punctuation, and usage problems that have been pointed out to me in previous essays?
24. \_\_\_\_\_Have I merely given a "reading" or have I presented an argument grounded in texts or evidence?
25. \_\_\_\_\_Have I borrowed any ideas from others without crediting my sources? That is, have I accidentally plagiarized?

# EXERCISES

*These exercises use the example of highlighting this handbook, making notes on what you read here, and turning those notes into a book review. The exercises assume you are taking notes on cards. You can emulate this process in a digital tool if you **really want to**, although I'd suggest beginning with paper and then adapting the processes to digital once you have the hang of them. You are free to pick another book to apply these exercises to processing. If you do choose to write a review describing your impressions of this book, feel free to send it to me! I'd be curious to see what you thought worked well and what might need another look. You can reach me at danallosso@icloud.com.*

### Exercise 1: Highlight

Use a writing implement or highlighter (if you're reading this in a paper format) or the highlight tool (if you're reading a pdf or e-book version) to mark the passages that jumped out at you as you were reading. Things you might want to highlight:

- Anything you didn't understand or wanted to get more information about,
- Something you want to remember,
- Something you agree or disagree with strongly

These highlights will later become the basis of your Source Notes. You want to include enough so you'll be able to accurately paraphrase and summarize the parts that interested you. But you don't want to overdo it. Usually 10% or 20% of the text is appropriate, if you're looking for main points or particularly interesting bits of evidence in the text (although it's always possible you'll *occasionally* run into an especially rich source and want to preserve more of it).

**Exercise 2: Make Source Notes**

Review your highlights. Pick the ones that still interest you. On a note card (or the digital equivalent of a card, if you're using an app) write a summary of the point made in the highlighted passage. Paraphrase rather than quoting, unless the passage contains something you're sure you are going to quote directly in your output. Even so, ALSO paraphrase the passage you quoted, to explain the point in your own words.

Consider how the point you have just summarized relates to your own interests or question or project? Give the card a short (ideally one-word) name that encapsulates the thought you have just recorded. This is the keyword that you think best explains the idea.

If you are working in a physical note system, add an Index entry and file it alphabetically in the Index.

Finally, thinking about the trains of thought already contained in your note system, decide where this new note will fit. The new idea should relate to the idea you pair it to, as a confirmation, counterpoint, modification, etc. Give the new note a number following the note you're attaching it to. For example, if the previous note was 1234, the new one will be 12345. If there is already a 12345, the new note follow you insert behind 1234 will be 1234a. Alternating letters and numbers will allow you to create an infinite number of branches, if necessary. Make a note of the card number on the Index card for the appropriate keyword (make a new Index card if you don't have one yet for that keyword).

These notes will be evidence to support your interpretations and arguments, which you will record on Point Notes. Relative to your highlights, you should once again be reducing the number of Source Notes you're taking the trouble to write, picking those you are reasonably sure will be useful on a particular question or project. You can always return to the source when you have a new question. Don't collect ideas you don't need right now, just for the sake of it.

### Exercise 3: Make Point Notes

This is where you are going to start recording your interpretations of the sources you've digested. The reason I called them "Point Notes" rather than Permanent or Main or Interpretive, was to remind myself that the purpose of them is to help me shift from recording and commenting on new facts I learn, to making my own points. These points can become topic sentences for paragraphs or even, if I continue to elaborate on them, thesis statements for projects.

Point Notes should also be numbered in the same scheme as the Source Notes, since the two will interact with each other. The evidence and data on Source Notes will feed your formulation of your points, and then will support those points when you present them in output.

Look at your Source Notes. Think about the implications of the information you have found for your project or question. Compare the ideas on different notes. Write down your thoughts and then, as you did on the Source Notes, add a keyword that best describes the thought on the card and a note ID number that follows the number of the note the new note will follow.

**Exercise 4: Outline**

This is where you get to see the payoff, when your notes come together to create a structure for output. In this case, review your Point Notes and arrange them into an argument about the book you read. Support your points using the Source Notes that led to them, and the citations from the text those were based upon.

Your outline can be as simple as a series of keywords and note IDs. That is basically what my outline for this book looked like. Then, as I was writing, I transcribed the points and source data, composing and then editing it so the argument flowed from one point to the next. Occasionally I'd have an additional thought as I was writing; I'd add it to the draft and write a new note about it. I think it worked out fairly well!

You will probably find that you have more than enough to say about the book, if you have worked through each of the exercises above. This is how an effective note system prepares you to create output. Often a concentration of notes on a particular topic will alert you that it's time to write some output. How cool is that? Rather than struggling to find a topic and something to say about it, you will be able to take advantage of the work you have already done as you read and processed new information.

Printed in Great Britain
by Amazon